D1086550

SANTA ALMOST GOT CAUGHT:

STORIES FOR THANKSGIVING, CHRISTMAS, AND THE NEW YEAR

KIRK H. NEELY
Emory Cash, Illustrator

ISBN: 978-145750-477-8

This book is printed on acid-free paper.

Printed in the United States of America

Unless otherwise indicated all scripture references in this book come from
THE HOLY BIBLE, NEW INTERNATIONAL VERSION®, NIV® Copyright © 1973, 1978,
1984, 2011 by *Biblica*, Inc.™ Used by permission. All rights reserved worldwide.

References are indicated KJV if taken from THE HOLY BIBLE: 1611 KING JAMES VERSION.

References are indicated NKJV if taken from THE NEW KING JAMES VERSION. Copyright ©
1982 by Thomas Nelson, Inc. Used by permission. All rights reserved.

Some of the anecdotal accounts in this book are true and are used with the permission of the per-
sons involved. All other accounts are composites of true situations. In many cases names and
details have been changed to protect the identity of specific individuals. In those instances, any
resemblance to any person living or dead is coincidental.

1681 union street
spartanburg, sc 29302
www.ourhomeplaceinc.com

First published by Dog Ear Publishing
4010 W. 86th Street, Ste H
Indianapolis, IN 46268
www.dogearpublishing.net

dog ear
PUBLISHING

Library of Congress Cataloging-in-Publication Data
Kirk H. Neely
Santa Almost Got Caught:Stories for Thanksgiving, Christmas, and the New Year/ Kirk H. Neely
    p.cm <http://p.cm> .
ISBN 978-145750-477-8
1. Neely, Kirk H.- Anecdotes 2.Southern Social Life and Customs - Anecdotes 3. Holidays - Anec-
dotes 4.Family - Holiday Celebrations 5. Holiday - Traditions 6.Kirk H. Neely - Memoir
I. Title

F277.S7N442009
975.729043 - dec22
2009027925

This book is dedicated to the memory of our son
Erik Hudson Neely
And to the memory of my father and mother,
Kirk Neely and Louise Hudson Neely.
Erik, Dad, and Mama loved the holidays.
It is the time of the year that I miss them most.

This book is dedicated to the memory of our son
Erik Hudson Neely
And to the memory of my father and mother,
Kirk Neely and Louise Hudson Neely.
Erik, Dad, and Mama loved the holidays.
It is the time of the year that I miss them most.

Also by Kirk H. Neely

Where to Go for Help, with Wayne E. Oates
Comfort and Joy: Nine Stories for Christmas
When Grief Comes: Finding Strength for Today and Hope for Tomorrow
A Good Mule Is Hard to Find and Other Tales from Red Clay Country
Banjos, Barbecue, and Boiled Peanuts
Neely Cousins
Hutson Heritage
By the Sea
Unto the Hills

Anthologies
Hub City Christmas
Stars Fell on Spartanburg
Outdoor Adventures in the Upcountry

TABLE OF CONTENTS

ANTICIPATING THE SEASON

1. Home for the Holidays 2
2. Can the Holidays be Holy Days? 5
3. Planning for the Season...8
4. The Inviting Table...11
5. The Empty Chair 14

THANKSGIVING

6. The First Thanksgiving 20
7. The Mayflower Story..23
8. A Tale of Two Birds 27
9. In Everything Give Thanks 30
10. A Kentucky Thanksgiving...33

ADVENT

11. The Meaning of Advent 38
12. A Season of Light...40
13. Surviving the Christmas Rush 44
14. Christmas Cards and Letters..46
15. The Christmas Rose..49
16. O Tannenbaum 52
17. The Joy of Stories 54
18. Christmas Carols in the Dark 57
19. The Prince of Peace..61
20. The Promise of Peace 63

CHRISTMAS

21. Keeping Christmas..68
22. Saint Nicholas and Santa Claus 71

23. Santa Almost Got Caught 74

24. Christmas Surprises 78

25. The Meaning of Gifts..80

26. The Best Gifts 82

27. Christmas at Croft 84

28. Searching for the Manger..88

29. Sending a Baby to Do a Messiah's Work 91

30. Madonna in Blue Jeans 94

31. G. I. Joe and Baby Jesus...96

THE NEW YEAR

32. The Twelve Days after Christmas.............................100

33. Out with the Old! In with the New! 102

34. On Making and Keeping Resolutions 104

35. A New Year's Treasure Hunt 107

36. Treasures of Snow 110

37. Jason's Story 113

EPIPHANY

38. The Meaning of Epiphany 116

39. The Epiphany Star 120

40. Personal Epiphany 124

41. Epiphany at Croft 126

42. Epiphany out of Africa 129

43. Epiphany at Ridgecrest 132

44. Epiphany at Hazelwood...135

Conclusion...139

Acknowledgements 140

About the Author 142

ANTICIPATING THE SEASON

1.

HOME FOR THE HOLIDAYS

The first December Clare and I were married, we wanted to return to visit our homes for Christmas. I was a first-year seminary student in Louisville, Kentucky. The first leg of our trip was to drive from Louisville to Spartanburg.

In those days the Interstate Highway System was a work in progress. It did not exist in the Southern Appalachian Mountains. Driving our old Chevrolet, we traveled east on U. S. Highway 60 through Frankfort and Lexington, Kentucky. Then we turned south down old U. S. Highway 25.

A light snow started falling about the time we left Lexington. The old road twists and turns through the mountains of Kentucky. By the time we drove through Richmond, Kentucky, heavy snow was falling. By Berea, the pavement was covered and traffic was slow. At Renfrow Valley we came to a complete stop. Traffic was a frozen gridlock.

The bridge over the Rockcastle River south of Livingston, Kentucky, was in treacherous condition. An eighteen-wheeler truck had jackknifed on the bridge, stopping traffic in both directions.

Motorists from north of the Ohio River became impatient with those of us from Dixie. The Yankees assumed that anybody whose vehicle sported a license plate from a Southern state did not know how to drive. Northerners tried to pass in the left lane and on the right shoulder. The result was that, when all was said and done, the four lanes of traffic were facing each other. The highway patrol troopers and big-rig wreckers could not even make their way to the accident because the cars were queued up bumper-to-bumper on the narrow mountain road. At the bridge, opposing lines of vehicles were at a standoff. It was a mess!

We sat in our car in one spot for eight hours. Clare had made gingerbread cookies to give to my family as their Christmas gift. We ate every morsel en route. I trudged through the snow to a little mountain diner to get coffee for us to enjoy with the gingerbread. Fortunately, we had a full tank of gasoline. I was able to occasionally crank the engine so we could reheat the car in order to stay warm. We improvised to meet our bathroom requirements. It was not the way I had envisioned my first Christmas with my new wife.

Finally, the logjam was broken. Traffic crept along slowly. The temperature was dropping. The road was frozen. Old U. S. Highway 25 winds across coal mining country, passing through towns like London, Corbin, and Williamsburg.

We pulled into London, Kentucky, after dark. Signs indicated that the National Guard Armory was open to travelers for the night. By the time we arrived, the emergency shelter was filled to capacity. So, we proceeded along the dark, icy highway to Corbin.

I knew that south of Williamsburg the road would be impassable over Jellico Mountain and extremely hazardous through LaFollette Gorge. We had to stop for the night. Every motel in Eastern Kentucky had a No Vacancy sign. Just south of Corbin, on the outskirts of town, I saw a motel next to Colonel Sander's Original Kentucky Fried Chicken Restaurant. Both the restaurant and the motel were closed. The neon No Vacancy sign glared into the cold night. I could see that half of the motel was completely dark, so I stopped anyway. I woke up the clerk who was on duty.

"We don't have any rooms," he said grumpily.

I replied, "I noticed that half the motel is dark. Those rooms are not occupied."

"Those are our summer units," he explained groggily. "They don't have any heat in them, and we've turned all the water off."

I asked, "What will you charge me for one room for one night, an unheated room?"

"You don't want to stay in an unheated room tonight," he said. "It's cold, and it's snowing."

"I don't want to drive over Jellico Mountain or go down into LaFollette Gorge in the dark either."

He agreed, "You're right."

He rented me a room at full price, which I gladly paid. He offered a space heater and gave us all the blankets we wanted. My young wife and I climbed into the bed and snuggled up with the blankets piled high. We got some much needed sleep.

The next morning, we resumed our journey, unshowered and disheveled. It was Christmas Eve. The Kentucky and Tennessee mountains were covered with snow. The landscape was like a Christmas card. It would have made a lovely scene viewed from a cozy cabin while sitting by a blazing fire sipping steaming coffee.

But, traveling by car was slow and hazardous. We stopped in Gatlinburg and bought tire chains for the drive over the Smoky Mountains. As we descended into North Carolina, we discovered to our relief that it had not snowed on the eastern side of the mountains.

We finally made it to the big Neely family party after supper was over. The festivities were breaking up. Members of the extended family were starting to leave.

The trip had been difficult for both of us, but especially for Clare. She was attending her first big Neely Christmas party. She had not seen most of those people since our wedding day the previous June. Imagine such a grueling journey, traveling to spend Christmas Eve with newly acquired in-laws. Arriving completely exhausted, unshowered, and tousled, she was mortified. Even the gingerbread cookies she had lovingly baked as a gift had all been devoured along a snowy mountain road.

The second leg of the trip was an early morning flight on Christmas Day to visit Clare's family in New Orleans.

When I reflect on the trip, it reminds me a little of the journey Mary and Joseph made to Bethlehem. The weary couple traveled over rough terrain by donkey to be counted and taxed by the Romans. Mary was to be in Joseph's town, no doubt ensconced with some of his kinfolks. She was great with child. They needed a place to stay, but there was no room in the crowded inn. Maybe with the assistance of an understanding innkeeper, they found the only place available, a place out back, a cave that served as a stable. On this night the cave became a delivery room. There, Jesus was born. It is the story of a Christmas journey.

The wisdom of Hebrew scripture records

> Two are better than one,
>   because they have a good return for their labor:
> If either of them falls down,
>   one can help the other up.
> But pity anyone who falls
>   and has no one to help them up.
> Also, if two lie down together, they will keep warm.
>   But how can one keep warm alone?
> Though one may be overpowered,
>   two can defend themselves.
> A cord of three strands is not quickly broken. (Ecclesiastes 4:9-12)

Every time I read these verses, I think about our marriage and that cold night in Kentucky. The scripture gives a wonderful description of what husbands and wives experience together. The third strand in the cord represents the presence of God in the marriage. The passage refers to physical as well as emotional and spiritual warmth.

Our snow adventure is an important holiday memory for us. It is also one of the reasons these holidays are so special for our family.

* * * * *

2.

CAN THE HOLIDAYS BE HOLY DAYS?

A health conscious businesswoman visited the gym to exercise as a part of her regular routine. She finished her daily workout by jogging several miles. In the winter months her running was done on a treadmill. One December morning the treadmill she was using went berserk. The control buttons, ordinarily used to slow and then stop the machine, were unresponsive. Instead of slowing down, the treadmill went faster. Frantically the woman punched the control panel, but to no avail. Her heart pounding, her breathing labored, she finally decided she would have to jump. Sprinting at a flat-out pace, she took a desperate leap of faith and fear. Though she was able to escape the renegade contraption, she landed hard on the concrete floor, fracturing her right wrist. She spent the holidays in a cast up to her elbow.

Something similar happens to many of us during the holidays. We are hijacked, not by a treadmill run amuck, but by the frenetic pace of activities. In fact, you probably don't have time to read this book. That's okay. Most of us move through the season between Thanksgiving and Epiphany at a breakneck pace. I don't think the holidays have always been so hectic. I don't believe the season has to be so stressful.

November and December are, for many, a favorite time of year. Our joy is enhanced by the return of cool crisp air, the aroma of wood smoke, and the flavors of delicious food. As the oldest of eight, I learned to treasure this time of year. In my childhood home, there was a palpable sense of anticipation and excitement as the holidays approached. My mother was the queen of celebration. She decorated our home and filled it with family and friends. Her coconut cake, lemon squares, and Kentucky Colonel chocolate bourbon balls alone were enough to draw a crowd.

I remember trekking through fields and woods on our old family farm with my dad, granddad, uncles, brothers, and cousins, searching for the perfect red cedar trees for Christmas. We gathered branches with bright red berries from holly trees. With a .22 rifle I had received as a gift for my twelfth Christmas, we shot mistletoe out of the tops of oak trees. Mama used all of the greenery to decorate.

Some of these traditions are distant memories. My wife, Clare, and I have learned that families must develop their own customs. The sage advice given to a bride planning her wedding may also apply to the holidays:

Something old, something new,
Something borrowed, something blue.

Something blue? The old Elvis Presley song "Blue Christmas" expresses the sadness many feel during the holidays. I learned long ago that these days may not be a season to be jolly. Nevertheless, the holidays can always be a time of comfort and joy.

This is a personal book. Many of the stories are from our family. When I lead a marriage enrichment retreat or speak to a group of parents, Clare always asks me to enter a disclaimer. We confront the same issues every other family must face. We struggle to find ways to make the holidays less frantic, too.

The days between Thanksgiving and the new year are filled with activity. Our pulse quickens with our pace. The season has become a stress-filled, busy time, so exhausting and exasperating that much of the joy is siphoned away. Though our Christmas cards and our sermons encourage us to remember the reason for the season, even that phrase becomes one more tired cliché.

Can these holidays become holy days?

The very word holiday means holy day. What a novel idea!

Holiness is a tainted concept. It has become identified with false piety, as in a holier-than-thou attitude. One of the commandments of Hebrew scripture is, "Be holy because I, the Lord your God, am holy" (Leviticus 19:2). Jesus includes this same teaching in the Sermon on the Mount. He said, "Be perfect, therefore, as your heavenly Father is perfect" (Matthew 5:48). It seems like an impossible expectation. The Greek word *teleios*, which is translated perfect, actually means complete. If the holidays are sacred days, we will not be left with the feeling that we are depleted, exhausted, or burned out. Rather, as the holidays conclude we will feel a sense of fulfillment.

To be holy also means to be different. It is a concept we need to reclaim for the holidays. We need to slow our pace, take a deep breath, and do things differently from the culture of frantic activity we see swirling around us.

Years ago, one of my brothers-in-law ordered a special license plate from the Department of Motor Vehicles here in South Carolina. *Hagios*, the Greek word for holy, was the inscription. Not long after he got the new plate mounted on his car, his vehicle was sideswiped at a busy intersection in our town. I saw his damaged car with two dented fenders, a scrape down one side, and the dented *Hagios* tag on the rear bumper. I was reminded that even those who strive for holiness are not exempt from the wear and tear of life.

We tend to draw a sharp line between what is sacred and what is secular. But, in truth, any life experience, when viewed through eyes of faith, can be seen as sacred.

The farm where we cut the cedar trees years ago was holy ground. But so, too, is the corner Christmas tree lot. This means that worship can be experienced anytime or anywhere. We anticipate a worship experience when we attend a community Thanksgiving service or enjoy a Christmas cantata. But worship can also happen when we pay attention to the words of a familiar carol or offer kindness to a child or a senior adult and receive a smile in return. If we are mindful of God's presence, holiness is always close at hand.

I hope you will read this book, even if you don't have time. You may read a chapter while waiting in a carpool line. Maybe you can enjoy a story while you rest on a bench in a crowded shopping mall. Open the book while flying in an airplane or riding on a city bus. You might even read while jogging on a treadmill, but please be careful!

As you read, remember that I have written with a prayer in my heart for you. I hope that you will feel some excitement about the holidays. I also hope that this time will be refreshing for you. Rather than being overfed physically or fed up emotionally, I pray that you will be nourished spiritually.

May your holiday season be less wearisome and more worshipful.

May these days be filled with less tension and more togetherness.

May you find less panic and more peace.

I hope *Santa Almost Got Caught* will help your holidays become holy days.

※ ※ ※ ※ ※

3.

PLANNING FOR THE SEASON

The choir director of a small church was frustrated and angry. At every rehearsal key members of the choir had been absent for one reason or another. Weary of their excuses, the director scolded the group for their lack of commitment.

Then the director complimented the pianist, "She's the only one I have been able to count on. She has been here for every rehearsal."

The pianist responded, "It was the least I could do, especially since I can't be here for the cantata on Sunday."

This is exactly the problem so many of us have. We spend an inordinate amount of time, money, and energy preparing for the holiday season, but when the important occasions arrive we are unable to fully participate.

Having been a pastor for forty-five years, I have learned to give choir directors and ministers of music a wide berth during the holidays. I have also learned that when it comes to promoting busyness, there are few offenders more to blame than the local church.

Years ago, a woman in a church that I served previously suggested that we offer a seminar to the congregation to address this very problem. We planned the class and called it "Making the Holidays Holy Days." The design of that class was the genesis of this book.

We started the seminar on the first Sunday night of November. I was taken aback by the large number of participants who showed up. Not only did we have a good response from our own members, but we also had visitors from churches of several different denominations. Those in attendance included adults from every age group. All were eager to discover a new way of making the holidays more meaningful for themselves and for their families.

At that first meeting I gave everyone a calendar that began with Thanksgiving week and extended through January 6. I identified the holiday season as the time beginning with Thanksgiving and continuing through Epiphany.

I asked each person to list on a separate sheet of paper what they really wanted for the holidays. Very few wrote down any material objects on their wish list. Almost all of the items dealt with the quality of relationships, the best use of time, the opportunity to be helpful to others, and ways to enhance spiritual growth.

With those objectives in mind, I invited each person to mark their calendar, making decisions ahead of time about those things they wanted to include in the holiday season. This meant, of course, also making decisions about what not to include. It was a most enlightening and helpful exercise.

For example, Clare and I decided that we simply could not attend every Christmas party to which we were invited. One couple having financial difficulties decided that they could not afford to give every relative a gift. To be intentional about the holidays may mean that we will not feel compelled to send a Christmas card to every person who sends one to us. We may discover the freedom to receive gifts from friends and acquaintances without feeling that we must reciprocate except with a gracious thank you.

The beginning of making the holidays holy days is a matter of establishing your values rather than being swept along by the tide of popular custom. It requires rethinking your priorities and developing your own traditions. In order to do this well you will need to take a little time to have conversation with your family. I believe you will be pleased with the results.

Take a fresh calendar that has nothing written in from Thanksgiving week until Epiphany, which always occurs on January 6. Make a list of what you really want to experience during the holidays. Beginning with the youngest child, let family members say one thing they would really like to do during the season. You may be surprised! When our children were young we heard these suggestions:

- Decorate the Christmas tree all together and have popcorn and hot chocolate.
- Go to the Christmas parade.
- Make Christmas cookies and take them to old people.
- Go Christmas caroling.
- Ride around town one night to look at the lights.
- Watch *It's a Wonderful Life* or *Miracle on 34th Street*.
- Go to a performance of Handel's *Messiah* where we can sing.
- Go see *The Nutcracker*.

As you fill in your calendar, be sure to include birthdays and anniversaries that are important to your family. Planning can reduce conflict. Remember you cannot do everything and still enjoy the holidays. Block out some days that are more relaxed. Give yourself some downtime.

There are some activities that you will have to do. Think carefully before adding them to your calendar. Usually the things we identify as obligations are the least satisfying. If you find yourself saying, "I should do this," or "I ought to do that," those might be the very activities that should or ought to be eliminated.

Include on your calendar a time to undecorate your home. Packing ornaments away takes time and care. My mother had a way of enticing us to help with the chore. After decorations came out of the boxes at the beginning of Advent, she hid small surprises in the empty containers. Then when the season was over, we children were more than glad to help in hopes that we would discover a treat.

Spread activities out as much as possible. Don't forget that the season stretches until after New Year's Day. As you will see later in this book, the twelve days after Christmas extend our celebration of the birth of Christ.

Begin and end your calendar time with a prayer. Ask God to help you do what the Apostle Paul called "redeeming the time" (Ephesians 5:16 KJV). That simply means to make the most of these days.

* * * * *

4.

THE INVITING TABLE

In the South good food plays an important role in holiday festivities. My ancestors living in humble cabins in the Tennessee hills found great joy in welcoming kith and kin to the family table. As a high school junior, during the week between Christmas and New Year's Day, I drove my grandfather to visit his Tennessee cousins. We went unannounced and were treated like royalty in every home.

My great, great grandfather's cabin still stands near Christiana. Just down the Shelbyville Pike in Bell Buckle, Myrtis Walls fed us one of the most memorable meals of my life. Fried chicken, country ham, cornbread, and bowls heaped full of vegetables kept us at the table for an hour or more.

As was the time-honored custom in Middle Tennessee even in 1960, the men were seated first. A kinswoman stood behind each man as we ate. Her task was to be sure there was no empty space on our plate. When a vacancy appeared, a feminine arm reached over our shoulder to plop down another delicious spoonful.

The boulevards at the plantation homes of my forebears in the Lowcountry of South Carolina were lined with pecan trees. Even modest homes had several pecan trees. The house where Clare and I live now has an expansive yard that features five pecan trees, all planted by my grandfather.

Each autumn the nuts were gathered from the ground by young and old alike. In the fall when families sat together in rocking chairs or on joggling boards on the front porch, cracking and picking pecans was a pastime.

Though they were plentiful, pecans were considered a delicacy. They were a popular snack roasted and salted, but they also were included in numerous recipes. My mother put them in apple salad, sweet potato soufflé, and banana bread. Pecan pie is the dessert of choice for a Southern Christmas.

Thanksgiving dinner featured a tender turkey, baked or smoked. Clare's mother made a delicious cranberry-apple bake that was a family favorite. Dressing and rice drenched with giblet gravy, several green vegetables, pickled peaches, and fried okra rounded out the main course. Pumpkin and sweet potato pies and coconut layer cake were the preferred desserts.

Sweet potatoes were a constant. Baked or candied, in casseroles, pies, or breads, yams were a part of holiday meals. During the Great Depression, Pappy raised sweet potatoes to sell and to serve as a staple food for his large family. A Neely family legend is that Mammy, of necessity, would prepare sweet potatoes three different ways for the same meal. There just wasn't much else to serve her family. In the South that was not uncommon even after the Depression. Uncle Buzz steadfastly declared that he would never eat another sweet potato. For the rest of his life, he remained true to his word!

Southerners enjoy adding seafood to holiday fare. Oyster dressing was always a part of Christmas dinner in Clare's home. We frequently include shrimp or scallops with our Christmas meal. For some families, crab cakes or she-crab soup is a prelude to the main course.

At the center of the table we placed a platter with the featured meat. This varied from family to family or from year to year. Favorites were beef tenderloin, wild goose, or a turkey deep-fried in peanut oil. A Christmas ham was traditional for many Southern families. My grandmother would soak a cured ham in apple juice overnight to remove some of the salt. She rubbed it with an orange, studded it with cloves, and basted it with apple cider.

Like many Southern families we gathered for a New Year's Day meal. It was as traditional as watching football bowl games. Pork chops, black-eyed peas or hoppin' john, collards or turnip greens, and cornbread was standard fare.

My dad was there to examine the dinner plates of all those gathered. He doled out a crisp two-dollar bill to anyone who ate their greens and black-eyed peas. Southern lore holds that anyone eating such a meal will enjoy prosperity in the year ahead. Dad gave us all a jump-start on the anticipated good fortune.

A pleasant blaze in the fireplace added the aroma of wood smoke to every holiday occasion. Family activities included walks in the woods, pickup basketball games, and, at Christmas time, the Neely Bowl Tag Football Game. The game became such a tradition that The Entertainment Sports Programming Network (ESPN) one year carried a brief story on the Neely Bowl.

Now, when Clare and I have our children and grandchildren with us for Thanksgiving, Christmas, or New Year's Day, we carry on some of these traditions. We enjoy simply being together. The children encourage me to tell a few stories. We may pull out the banjo or the guitar or gather around the piano to sing.

Pappy advised, "Don't get married and hire a cook. Just marry the cook!"

I certainly heeded that advice. We always enjoy good food, much of it traditional. Most of all we are grateful for what we have to enjoy together.

Clare's parents and grandparents, as well as my parents and grandparents, knew the fine points of Southern hospitality. Guests were always welcomed at the table. Setting another place was not considered a bother, it was a privilege. Over the years, we have often invited others to share our holiday meals. Usually, we have included those who would otherwise be alone: a friend newly widowed, a person recently divorced, or a student far from home.

One especially meaningful meal occurred on a Friday night in Advent.

A Jewish rabbinical student from New York was visiting in our home as was our young friend from North Carolina. They asked Clare if they could prepare a Shabbat meal in our kitchen and observe the Sabbath around our table. We readily agreed.

As plans were being made, we received a phone call from a nephew who was working in our town with AmeriCorps. He had twelve young people who were on his work team. He wanted them to enjoy a good home cooked meal. So they were all invited.

Clare and I arranged tables all the way across our dining room, into the den, and into our living room as one long continuous board. Clare broke out her Mitchell family heirloom linen and damask tablecloths and napkins for the occasion.

The Jewish student presided. He and his new friend planned the menu, did all of the shopping, and prepared every morsel, including poached salmon, challah bread baked from scratch, and all the fixings. The unique assemblage observed a Shabbat meal together.

At every meal in my grandparent's home, Pappy said the blessing. It was always the same. "Lord, make us thankful for these and all thy many blessings. For Christ's sake. Amen."

Dad and Mama remembered to say the blessing around the table as did Clare's parents. Clare and I have continued that tradition. We have a blessing at every meal. When our grandchildren are present, our custom is to allow them to request their favorite mealtime prayer.

Sometimes we sing the "Johnny Appleseed Blessing." Sometimes it is the "Superman Blessing Cheer." At other times it is a prayer that is spontaneous.

And we are thankful.

* * * * *

5.
THE EMPTY CHAIR

The headline caught my eye, "Man Spends Christmas Eve in Septic Tank." In an article dated December 26, 2007, the Associated Press carried the humorous and frightening story.

Robert Schoff, a 77-year-old man from Des Moines, Iowa, spent part of Christmas Eve stuck upside down in the opening of his septic tank, with his head inside and his feet kicking in the air above.

"I don't think I could have stood staying in there much more," he said as he recovered from his ordeal. "It wasn't good! It was a stinky holiday! I'll tell you what," Schoff said on Christmas Day, "It was the worst Christmas Eve I've ever had."

Schoff reached into the tank on Christmas Eve in an effort to clear a clogged drain. He lost his balance and became wedged in the opening. The elderly Schoff shouted for help, but in this upside-down position his voice was muffled. It was more than an hour before his wife, Toni, walked by a window and noticed his feet flailing in the air.

"I saw these kicking feet. I ran to him, but I couldn't get him out," Mrs. Schoff said.

She called 911. County sheriff's deputies arrived and yanked her husband out of the tank.

"I thought it was the end of my life," Schoff said.

What a way to go that would have been!

For all of our careful planning, the holidays often confront us with unexpected crises. I spent most of one Christmas Eve in the surgical chair of an ear, nose, and throat specialist. I had a hemorrhage resulting in a severe nosebleed. The physician cauterized and packed my sinuses with gauze for well over two hours. It was not the best Christmas Eve for me, for the physician, or for our families. Still, it was not as bad as Robert Schoff's plight.

The heightened stress of the season seems to make some folks more accident-prone. I have a friend who spent the last two weeks of December on crutches after stepping in a hole while caroling in his neighborhood.

By far the most difficult holidays are those times when we are separated from loved ones. The painful absence is symbolized by an empty chair at the family table.

I vaguely remember Christmas 1948 when I was four years old. The entire Neely family gathered on Christmas Eve for our annual Christmas dinner. Following the meal, we recited the story of Jesus' birth from Luke 2. We sang Christmas carols, Pappy led a prayer, and we exchanged gifts. That night my little sister Beth and I stayed with Mammy and Pappy.

Mama was at the hospital giving birth to her third child. My brother Bill was born on December 24 that year. According to my aunts and uncles, I spent much of that Christmas looking for Mama. Jesus was born, and Santa Claus came, but Mama was not there.

The holidays are frequently tinged with grief. The season has often been a bittersweet experience for our family, a mixture of joy and sadness. In fact, when you are a part of a large family, you learn that life itself is a dichotomy. Ambivalent feelings about any event abound. Humor and sadness, laughter and tears, mingle on many family gatherings.

In the Neely family, it is rarely possible to have everybody together for any occasion. I remember a birthday party for one my brothers-in-law. Most of the family was present except for the honoree. He had suddenly come down with the flu and was confined to quarters while the rest of us partied on.

Some of us who are physicians and ministers are frequently called away from family events to fulfill our responsibilities in the community. So, we have learned to be grateful for those who can gather. Celebrations still happen even when there are empty chairs at the table.

In my grandparent's family, there were several holiday seasons when three sons and a son-in-law were serving in World War II. At the same time, another son and his family were far away on the mission field in South America.

At almost every celebration, a few are absent. An expectant mother and her family may be unable to travel during the holidays. Sometimes a student is traveling on foreign study. Our son Scott spent his junior year at Wofford College living with a family in France. The next year he was in India during the holidays. The Christmas after our son Erik's death, our son Kris traveled aboard a hammock boat on the Amazon River.

I will never forget the December when three different times in three consecutive weeks I stood beside an open grave with grieving parents as tiny caskets were lowered into the ground. The deaths of those children meant that their bereaved families would mourn a painful absence during the holidays. One of those tiny coffins was for our infant niece, Katherine. Our entire family was affected by her death.

I know of a home where the decorated Christmas tree remains in the living room throughout the year. The tree is, of course, artificial, but the life situation that prompted the custom is real. At the beginning of the Christmas season, after they had put up their tree, the onset of a terminal illness besieged the husband and father. At the end of the holidays, they just could not muster the energy to take the tree down. Over time, their reason for leaving their Christmas tree in place changed. "My husband got sick the first week of December and died twenty months later in August," said the widow. "The whole time he was dying we enjoyed the tree together. It gave us a feeling of peace and comfort. So, we decided to just leave it up all the time."

Clare and I have experienced some of the joy and the sorrow that Christmas can bring. Our oldest child, Mike, was born on Christmas Day in 1970. As we awaited his birth, the season of Advent was filled with anticipation and hope. The uncertainty and apprehension of becoming new parents was part of our emotional mix. Christmas was a day of fulfillment for us.

Thirty years later, our second son, Erik, died two weeks before Thanksgiving. Christmas that year was a season of deep grief for us. Still, we were able to find a measure of peace and joy mingled with our tears.

November in South Carolina is usually a mild month. Not until after Thanksgiving does the weather begin to really feel like winter. Erik died on November 15, 2000, in Charleston. The temperature in the Lowcountry was warm that day. We returned from Charleston to our home in the Upstate with the sky bright and sunny. But the day of the funeral dawned grey, cold, and damp. Temperatures continued to fall through the day. By the time we arrived at the church for the funeral, light snow was falling. When we went to the cemetery for the committal service, the ground was covered with snow.

Some expressed regret that the weather was inclement on the day of our son's service. We felt differently. In our imagination, we thought that Erik had put in a request to the Almighty. "Lord, you know this will be a hard day for my family. Could you do something to surprise them?"

We viewed the snow as a symbol of hope. We interpreted the snow as a gentle touch from God, a gift of grace in our grief. Many of the Christmas cards and Christmas presents we received that year included a snow theme. As Christmas approached, we decided to decorate our Christmas tree with only snowflakes and snow ornaments. Hand-cut snowflakes adorned our windows.

In Louisa May Alcott's *Little Women*, Jo expresses this impending grief in the face of the illness of her sister Beth and the absence of their father during the Civil War. "Our dear Beth came back to us, although the fever had weakened her heart forever. We did not know then that a shadow had fallen. We prepared for another Christmas without Father."

One of the truths that Clare and I have learned is that grief, especially following the death of a young person, casts a long shadow. Our grief for Erik lingers and is heightened in every holiday season. Therefore his name and our sense of loss crop up in our lives and throughout these pages.

But there is another truth.

Our widowed daughter-in-law, June, majored in art at Furman University. She is an accomplished artist. After Erik's death, June painted a stunning watercolor. It was a table set for a party, but it included an empty chair, a poignant reminder of absence. The painting is also a vivid depiction of hope. On the table are party hats. Streamers and balloons adorn the room.

The chair is empty. The celebration continues.

*****

THANKSGIVING

6.

THE FIRST THANKSGIVING

We may all be familiar with the longstanding tradition that the first Thanksgiving on American soil occurred in 1621 at Plymouth Plantation. But, at least four earlier accounts of Europeans holding an observance of thanksgiving on the American continent have been documented.

- September 8, 1565, Spanish explorers and Timucua Indians celebrated a day of thanksgiving in St. Augustine, Florida.
- September 23, 1578, Martin Frobisher held a formal ceremony of thanksgiving in Newfoundland to express gratitude for surviving the long journey in an unsuccessful attempt to find a Northwest Passage to the Pacific Ocean.
- April 30, 1598, Spanish conquistadores and Native Americans south of El Paso, Texas, held a thanksgiving observance.
- December 4, 1619, English settlers in the Virginia colony of Jamestown set aside a day of thanksgiving when ships arrived with food and supplies.

While details are sparse, these occasions of European thanksgiving preceded the celebration at Plymouth Colony in 1621. None of them, though, qualifies as the first Thanksgiving.

I would contend that the first Thanksgiving took place long before recorded history. Before the establishment of formal religious observances, ancient people believed that spirits caused their crops to grow. Harvest festivals including expressions of gratitude were held by the ancient Greeks, Romans, Hebrews, Chinese, and Egyptians. Throughout history humankind has celebrated bountiful harvests with ceremonies of gratitude.

A specific provision for a thanksgiving offering among the ancient Hebrews is described in detail in the Bible in Leviticus 7. Later in Hebrew history, families also celebrated a harvest festival called *Sukkoth*. Taking place each autumn, *Sukkoth* has been celebrated for over 3000 years. The festival is known by two alternate names: the Feast of the Tabernacles and the Feast of Ingathering. *Sukkoth* is named for the booths that Moses and the Israelites lived in as they wandered the desert for forty years before they reached the Promised Land. *Sukkoth* begins five days after *Yom Kippur*, which is the Day of Atonement, the most solemn day of the Jewish year.

In North America, Thanksgiving was celebrated long before the arrival of European colonists. Most Americans understand that the stories surrounding Thanksgiving at Plymouth Colony are romanticized. Few Native Americans believe this day meant that peace and harmony had become a reality between the Indians and the Pilgrims. Most native people regard the event as the beginning of an onslaught that would reduce the number of Indians from more than one million to about 200,000 by the beginning of the 20th Century.

The day known as Thanksgiving has been accepted as a legal holiday by some Native Americans because the idea of a day to give thanks is such a strong part of their own traditions and culture.

Writing for *The Christian Science Monitor* on November 27, 2002, Elizabeth Armstrong quotes Linda Coombs, associate director of the Wampanoag program at Plymouth Plantation. "There are *wopila*, giving thanks celebrations, all of the time among the Indian people of the Great Plains. A son or daughter returning home from war is an occasion for a *wopila* celebration. A *wopila* to celebrate a high school or college graduation is common. When someone recovers from an accident or a serious illness, a *wopila* ceremony is held."

So the idea of a day of thanksgiving has been a part of Native American cultures for centuries. The fact that it is a national holiday for all Americans blends well with Native American traditions.

Coombs continues, "We as native people traditionally have thanksgivings as a daily, ongoing thing. Every time anybody went hunting or fishing or picked a plant, they would offer a prayer of acknowledgment."

The wisdom sayings among Native Americans encourage a daily attitude of thanksgiving. A simple prayer by an author lost to memory expresses it well. "We give thanks for unknown blessings already on their way."

In a sense, each day can be a day of thanksgiving. Greeting the sunrise at dawn, marveling at the sunset at close of day, and innumerable other blessings can each prompt an attitude of appreciation.

The following is an Iroquois thanksgiving prayer:

We return thanks to our mother, the earth,
Which sustains us.
We return thanks to the rivers and streams,
Which supply us with water.
We return thanks to all herbs,
Which furnish medicines for the cure of our diseases.
We return thanks to the moon and stars,
Which have given to us their light when the sun was gone.

We return thanks to the sun,
That has looked upon the earth with a beneficent eye.
Lastly, we return thanks to the Great Spirit,
in whom is embodied all goodness,
And who directs all things for the good of her children.

Biblical wisdom counsels a similar mindset.

"This is the day the Lord has made; we will rejoice and be glad in it" (Psalm 118:24 NKJV).

"Because of the Lord's tender mercies we are not consumed, for his compassions never fail. They are new every morning; great is your faithfulness" (Lamentations 3:22-23 Author's Paraphrase).

When we adopt this attitude, every day becomes a day of thanksgiving.

✳ ✳ ✳ ✳ ✳

7.
THE MAYFLOWER STORY

More than thirty years ago in Boston I visited a replica of the *Mayflower*, the vessel that brought the Pilgrims to the shores of the New World. I was struck by how small the ship was. The thought of crowding 102 people on a boat 128-feet-long and enduring an ocean voyage of sixty-six days is mind-boggling.

In the middle of the Atlantic, the small *Mayflower* was swept into a fierce storm. A tremendous wave broke across the deck of the ship, splintering boards and fracturing one of the main beams. With Captain Christopher Jones shouting orders above the roar of the raging sea, the crew employed a large iron screw jack to lift the broken beam and the sagging deck back into place. After inspecting the repairs, Captain Jones decided that the ship's hull was sound. The journey continued.

The storm at sea was yet another event in a long history of difficulties faced by the Pilgrims. A decade after removing themselves from the Church of England, the Separatists lived as exiles in Holland. The Puritans, as they were also known, negotiated for three years before obtaining the necessary sponsor to establish a colony in the New World. Only eight Separatist families were prepared to make the pilgrimage across the ocean. They were seeking religious freedom.

Thinking that the group was too small to survive, the Virginia Company recruited volunteers to join the voyage. The Puritans referred to these recruits as strangers. The passengers — strangers and pilgrims, soldiers and sailors, recruits with their families, and eight Separatist families — made the perilous voyage together.

The *Mayflower*'s intended destination was the Jamestown Colony. Whether or not Captain Jones knew the ship was off course is unknown; but at sunrise on November 9, 1620, the high ground of Cape Cod was sighted. The *Mayflower* would have to sail three more weeks to reach Jamestown.

The decision was made to go as far south as the mouth of the Hudson River, just inside the boundary of the Virginia Company's claimed land. A few hours later, another storm, roaring out of Nantucket Sound, drove the small ship back to the north. The *Mayflower* found refuge just inside the tip of Cape Cod at the safe harbor now known as Provincetown.

One of the strangers onboard was Steven Hopkins. His wife had given birth to a son at sea on the *Mayflower* only a few days after the fierce storm that broke the crossbeam. The infant was appropriately named Oceanus.

Hopkins had overheard mutinous talk among some of the strangers. They grumbled that if the *Mayflower* landed outside of the Virginia Company's territory, the authority of the colony would not be legally binding upon them.

The Separatists heard the rumor. Their leaders — William Brewster, William Bradford, John Carver, and Edward Winslow — wrote out a statement of self-government. The Separatists persuaded the others on board to sign the document. Before anyone set foot on solid ground, forty-one men, strangers as well as pilgrims, had signed the Mayflower Compact.

Over the following weeks, the *Mayflower* continued to explore the inner curve of Cape Cod, searching for a suitable harbor. Finally on December 21, the trustworthy vessel found a haven at Plymouth. By Christmas Day, a holiday the Puritans did not observe, construction on the first buildings had begun. While homes were being built, the people continued to live aboard the cramped *Mayflower*.

The first winter in the New World was severe, and disease was rampant. Pneumonia and scurvy decimated the ranks of the colonists. By spring, fifteen of the eighteen wives had died, as had five of the twenty-eight children. Nineteen of the twenty-nine hired men and fifteen of the thirty sailors died from hard work in the harsh weather. Only five Pilgrim men and eight strangers remained alive. Teenager Priscilla Mullins lost her entire family.

The bereavement and hardships of that winter bound strangers and Pilgrims together. A hardened soldier, Miles Standish tended the sick alongside Separatist William Brewster. Sneering sailors and praying Puritans now shared a common suffering.

On March 16, a tall, half-naked man walked into the circle of startled villagers. He introduced himself as Samoset. He spoke only a little English. So, he left in frustration. Three days later, Samoset returned with Squanto, who knew English very well. These two Native Americans were largely responsible for the survival of the depleted colony. Perhaps aware of the hardships the colonists had endured, the Indians taught the Europeans how to hunt and fish.

Following the death of Governor William Carver in April 1621, the *Mayflower* set sail for the return voyage to Europe. The fifty people of Plymouth Colony, more than half of them children, were left in America. Priscilla Mullins became the bride of John Alden. Widows and widowers were united in marriage.

Massasoit, Chief of the Narragansett tribe, befriended the Pilgrims. A treaty signed by both groups kept the peace for fifty-four years, until Massasoit's death. Native Americans advised the colonists on agricultural methods that enabled the Plymouth community to enjoy a good harvest. On December 13, 1621, a three-day feast was planned. Massasoit came with ninety Indians. We often refer to that feast as the first Thanksgiving.

At that gathering, William Bradford read Psalm 107. If we read the Psalm closely, we can understand why Bradford selected it.

A portion of that Psalm reads:

1 Oh, give thanks to the Lord, for he is good!
    For his mercy endures forever.
2 Let the redeemed of the Lord say so...

4 They wandered in the wilderness in a desolate way;
    They found no city to dwell in.
5 Hungry and thirsty,
    Their soul fainted in them.
6 Then they cried out to the Lord in their trouble,
    And he delivered them out of their distresses.
7 And he led them forth by the right way,
    That they might go to a city for a dwelling place...

23 Those who go down to the sea in ships,
    Who do business on great waters,
24 They see the works of the Lord,
    And his wonders in the deep.
25 For he commands and raises the stormy wind,
    Which lifts up the waves of the sea.
26 They mount up to the heavens,
    They go down again to the depths;
    Their soul melts because of trouble.
27 They reel to and fro, and stagger like a drunken man,
    And are at their wits' end.
28 Then they cry out to the Lord in their trouble,
    And he brings them out of their distresses.

29 He calms the storm,
   So that its waves are still.
30 Then they are glad because they are quiet;
   So he guides them to their desired haven...

39 When they are diminished and brought low
   Through oppression, affliction, and sorrow,
40 He pours contempt on princes,
   And causes them to wander in the wilderness where there is no way;
41 Yet he sets the poor on high, far from affliction,
   And makes their families like a flock.
42 The righteous see it and rejoice,
   And all iniquity stops its mouth.
43 Whoever is wise will observe these things,
   And they will understand the lovingkindness of the Lord.
                                              (Psalm 107 NKJV)

Four times in Psalm 107 the refrain is repeated, "Oh, that men would give thanks to the Lord for his goodness, and for his wonderful works to the children of men!" (Psalm 107: 8, 15, 21, 31 NKJV).

The people of the *Mayflower* serve as an example for all of us. We learn from them that our deepest expressions of gratitude may come in the midst of our greatest difficulties.

* * * * *

8.
A TALE OF TWO BIRDS

Born into the family of a Boston candle maker, Benjamin Franklin became one of the most famous Americans of his time. As a founder of the United States of America, he had many good ideas and at least one bad one.

Franklin helped to establish a new nation and to define the structure and function of American government. The Philadelphia statesman played a major role in crafting our Declaration of Independence and our Constitution.

Franklin's inventions reveal a man of varied interests, many talents, boundless energy, and great curiosity. Ben had poor eyesight. Tired of constantly taking his glasses off and on, he cut two pairs of spectacles in half. Putting half of each lens in single frames, he invented bifocals. I am grateful for his invention every single day.

My family and I deeply appreciate the fact that Ben Franklin founded the first public lending library. What a great idea!

Franklin learned much about ships during his eight voyages across the Atlantic Ocean. He suggested dividing a ship's hold into watertight compartments so that if a leak occurred in one, the water would not spread throughout and sink the ship.

In colonial America, people warmed their homes with an open fireplace, a dangerous practice that burned a lot of wood. Ben invented an iron furnace that used less wood and allowed for warmer, safer homes. His invention is still called a Franklin Stove. In the same vein, Ben also established the first fire department and the first fire insurance company. Think of that the next time you see one of the big trucks rushing to a fire.

As Postmaster, Franklin mapped mail delivery routes. He invented a simple odometer. When attached to his carriage, it allowed him to measure the distance of postal routes accurately.

Inventor, businessman, writer, scientist, musician, humorist, diplomat, civic leader, international celebrity, and ladies' man, Ben Franklin was a genius.

Like most brilliant folk, Ben Franklin had a few crazy notions. The story of Ben's famous kite is well known. Rigging a kite with wire and a brass key, he flew it in a thunderstorm. Not a good idea. Because of him, meteorologists now refer to thunderstorms as electrical storms. Out of his hair-raising experiment came Ben's invention of the lightning rod.

Franklin had one very bad idea that could have altered the course of history and changed the celebration of Thanksgiving as we now know it. Ben proposed to Congress that the wild turkey be designated as our national bird. Thank goodness the distinguished group of legislators saw fit to overrule the patriot from Pennsylvania. In their wisdom, Congress made the bald eagle our national bird, not the wild turkey.

Imagine how our lives might have been different if Benjamin Franklin had prevailed and the turkey, rather than the eagle, had become the symbol of our great nation. We can all be glad that Ben Franklin did not have his way.

- Our coins might be minted with turkeys on the reverse side rather than with eagles. A flip of the coin might require a call, "Heads or turkeys?"
- The Great Seal of the United States of America might display the image of a wild turkey instead of a bald eagle.
- The professional football team in Ben Franklin's City of Brotherly Love might not be the Philadelphia Eagles, but the Philadelphia Turkeys.
- When Neil Armstrong and Buzz Aldrin landed the *Apollo 11 Lunar Module* on the surface of the moon, we might have heard the radio transmission, "Tranquility base here. The turkey has landed."
- The Boy Scouts of America might never have become the character developing organization that it is today. Scouts might not be as motivated to make their way through the ranks if the highest award were the Turkey Scout Award. To call a young man a Turkey Scout just doesn't have the same ring as the honor of being an Eagle Scout.

The turkey season that begins on April Fool's Day might be quite controversial if camouflaged hunters, armed with turkey calls and rifles, were preying on our national bird. I have a notion that Thanksgiving Day might be a different kind of celebration if families who gathered at Grandma's house were praying over and feasting on our national symbol. We can be grateful that the eagle is on our coins and the turkey is on our tables.

Both ornithology and theology point to the eagle as a rare bird. The eagle is a symbol of strength and achievement, representing the qualities of clear vision and vigilant protection.

The Bible includes multiple references to the eagle. Turkeys, however, are never mentioned.

Perhaps you will gather with your loved ones on Thanksgiving Day to enjoy a turkey dinner. Before the meal, take a moment to give thanks for two birds, the turkey and the eagle. You might choose to read Psalm 103, a beautiful prayer about the blessings of God that mentions the eagle. Or perhaps you would enjoy the words of the prophet Isaiah in one of the best-loved references to the eagle:

> But they that wait upon the Lord shall renew their strength;
> they shall mount up with wings as eagles;
> they shall run, and not be weary;
> and they shall walk, and not faint. (Isaiah 40:31 KJV)

True thanksgiving is as rare and as endangered as the eagle. Thanksgiving has nothing to do with the bird on our platter. It has everything to do with the prayer in our heart.

* * * *

9.

IN EVERYTHING GIVE THANKS

Just before Thanksgiving in 2000, our twenty-seven-year-old son, Erik, died suddenly. Some people lamented that our Thanksgiving that year would be ruined. They were concerned that our Thanksgivings would be forevermore overshadowed with sorrow.

We found just the opposite to be true. Beyond the parades, the football games, and the turkey, Thanksgiving has become more meaningful for us.

Thanksgiving in this country has often been linked with times of hardship. The first Thanksgiving, observed in 1621 by the Pilgrims, followed a severe winter of deprivation and death.

The Thanksgiving Proclamation of George Washington in 1789, during the first year of his presidency, encouraged a fledging country "to acknowledge with grateful hearts the many and signal favors of Almighty God."

In 1863, at the height of the Civil War, President Abraham Lincoln issued his Thanksgiving Proclamation. Even with a country divided in crisis, the President remembered the blessings of God.

> They are the gracious gifts of the Most High God...It has seemed to me fit and proper that they should be solemnly, reverently, and gratefully acknowledged as with one heart and one voice by the whole American People. I do therefore invite my fellow citizens in every part of the United States...to set apart and observe the last Thursday of November next, as a day of Thanksgiving and Praise to our beneficent Father who dwelleth in the Heavens. And I recommend to them that while offering up the ascriptions justly due to Him for such singular deliverances and blessings, they do also, with humble penitence...commend to His tender care all those who have become widows, orphans, mourners or sufferers in the lamentable civil strife in which we are unavoidably engaged...

Our deepest expressions of gratitude come in the midst of our greatest difficulties. I heard a story thirdhand that is a poignant illustration of that truth.

A pastor and his wife from eastern North Carolina suffered the loss of their young adult son. One dark, rainy night, he was badly injured in an automobile accident. At the emergency room, the bleak diagnosis of severe trauma to the head prompted transfer to the neurological intensive care unit. Over the next few hours, a team of physicians concurred that the young man was brain dead. The father knew from his experience as a pastor that his son's death was imminent.

The parents were reminded that their son had indicated a desire to be an organ donor. When they looked at their son's driver's license, his wishes were confirmed. Arrangements were made and paperwork completed so that when death came, as many organs as possible could be preserved for transplants.

The following day, the decision to remove all life-support was made. The young man died within a matter of minutes. His organs were distributed to other hospitals where patients were awaiting a transplant.

Organ donation protocol allows for the deceased person's next of kin to know the names of those who are given the transplants if both the donor's family and the recipients agree. The pastor and his wife wanted to know the people who had been given their son's organs. Three of those agreed. The names and addresses were delivered to the couple in the spring. The pastor and his wife decided to invite these three transplant survivors to a meal at their home on the Saturday before Thanksgiving Day.

At the appointed time, the organ recipients and their spouses arrived at the couple's home. The pastor and his wife greeted and welcomed each one at the door. Together they gathered to enjoy a Thanksgiving meal.

Years later, the pastor related the story of their Thanksgiving experience.

> As we stood in a circle to have the blessing, the woman who had received our son's heart moved between my wife and me. As we reached out to hold hands during the blessing, the woman placed my fingers on her left wrist and my wife's hand on her right wrist. My wife and I could feel the lady's pulse. We realized that we were feeling the pumping of our son's strong heart, now transplanted into this woman's body.
>
> Another of our guests, a gentleman, asked if he might say grace. We agreed and heard his prayer, blessing our home and us and giving thanks for the life of our son. We were aware that his voice was strong because our son's lungs had been transplanted into his chest.
>
> Sitting across the table from us during the meal was a young woman. We realized that she looked at us with steel blue eyes that were once the eyes of our son.
>
> It was the most meaningful Thanksgiving we have ever had. Of course, we were still grieving. But we also had discovered hope. Our son had died, but he had literally given a part of himself to our guests around the table. Our hearts were filled with gratitude as we met the people whose lives had been so changed by our son.

The Apostle Paul wrote to the early Christian community, "give thanks in all circumstances" (I Thessalonians 5:16). His instruction is not easy to follow. We find some comfort, though, in noting that Paul did not say that we are to be thankful for every circumstance. Rather, within the difficulties of life, we are to find reason for gratitude. When life is hard, as it is for everyone, we have a tendency to become bitter and cynical. If we seek reasons to be grateful, even our most difficult experiences can be transformed.

Thanksgiving is the response of a grateful heart.

* * * * *

10.
A KENTUCKY THANKSGIVING

The fourth Thursday of November, for most of us, is a time for reflection, for gratitude, even for nostalgia. One of my most important Thanksgiving memories is a Kentucky Thanksgiving with Bobby.

Bobby was fourteen years old and large for his age, but shy and withdrawn. His severe acne, unkempt hair, broken front tooth, smudged glasses, and distant stare were external evidence of a troubled mind and a broken heart.

Bobby was a patient in the Adolescent Unit at Central State Hospital, a mental hospital in Anchorage, Kentucky, where I worked as a chaplain. Though Bobby was diagnosed as being chronically depressed and borderline schizophrenic, he had moments when his intellectual functioning exceeded all expectations. Bobby was one of the patients who had prompted the comment, "The main difference between the staff and the patients in this hospital is that the patients get better."

As Thanksgiving approached during those golden autumn days in Kentucky, the staff in the Adolescent Unit was delighted to learn that most of the teenage patients would be given a three-day home visit for the holiday. The treatment team determined that Bobby, however, was not ready to function for three days away from the hospital. His home situation had been assessed as being so dysfunctional that he could be allowed no more than a one-day visit accompanied by a hospital staff member. If Bobby went home for Thanksgiving Day, he would have to return that same night.

Other staff members had looked forward to having Thanksgiving Day away from the hospital, so I volunteered to accompany Bobby to his home in the mountains of Kentucky for the day. The social worker contacted his mother and his grandparents to plan the visit. I arranged to drive Bobby to his mother's house for Thanksgiving dinner and bring him back to the hospital before nightfall. Clare and I decided to have our family Thanksgiving meal after I returned.

Thanksgiving Day dawned clear and cold. I met Bobby at the Adolescent Unit early, wondering what this visit to his home would mean to him. Those dark, vacant eyes, almost concealed behind dirty glasses, revealed no excitement. The sunny Thanksgiving morning and the beautiful Kentucky landscape made a scenic trip of our three-hour drive through the bluegrass horse country and into the mountains.

Though I attempted several times to strike up a conversation with Bobby about his family and their usual Thanksgiving celebration, Bobby responded with silence. His only conversation was a running commentary on the make and model of every automobile on the highway. He knew details about many of the cars, such as engine size and horsepower. The only significant exchange between us was his assertion that I had not made a wise selection when I had purchased my used Jeep. I should have chosen a Ford Mustang, he advised.

When we arrived in the coal mining town, Bobby directed me to his mother's house. A note of anticipation arose in his voice as we approached the modest home. The frame house suffered from neglect. Shingles were missing from the roof, and paint was peeling from the wooden siding. The screen door had fallen completely off the hinges.

Bobby said, "Her truck is gone. She's not here." Though his face showed no emotion, his voice disclosed disappointment. Bobby did not knock on the door. He just opened the unlocked door to search the house. No one was home.

"Could she be at your grandparents' house?" I asked.

"We can see," replied Bobby.

We drove in silence for several miles on a winding back road to his grandparent's home. The log house, perched on a mountainside, showed no sign of life.

"Maybe we missed them," suggested Bobby.

We took the twisted trip back into town to his mother's home. Still, no one was there. I offered to buy Thanksgiving dinner for the two of us, not knowing where I could find a restaurant, much less a restaurant open on the holiday.

Bobby shook his head refusing my offer. "I'll fix something," he said.

Inside the small kitchen, I watched as my fourteen-year-old host opened the refrigerator. It was well stocked with beer, but food was sparse. Bobby took out bologna and a bowl of cold grits. In a large iron skillet, he fried thick slices of bologna. In the remaining grease, he browned slices of cold grits. I fixed two glasses of water.

We sat in ladder-back chairs at an old card table. Following my own Thanksgiving tradition, I quoted Psalm 100 and offered a blessing. I hoped that Bobby would talk about his feelings, but he did not. We ate our fried bologna and grits in almost total silence. We cleaned up the dishes together. When it was time to leave, we closed the door, leaving it unlocked as we had found it.

The three-hour drive back to the institution seemed interminable. Again, our only conversation was about automobiles. At one point, I tried to allow Bobby to speak about his hurt. "I'm sorry we didn't get to be with your family."

Bobby replied stoically, "It's okay." Then he commented on a passing Pontiac.

Just before sunset, Bobby and I climbed the back stairs to the Adolescent Unit. A child care worker unlocked the door to allow for our entry.

As I prepared to leave, Bobby threw his arms around my neck in an awkward bear hug. Then he said, "This is the best Thanksgiving I have ever had."

As I walked back to my Jeep, I had tears in my eyes. I drove home to celebrate Thanksgiving with Clare and our family.

On Thanksgiving Day, our family repeats together the words of the Bible, "Enter into his gates with thanksgiving, and into his courts with praise: be thankful unto him, and bless his name" (Psalm 100:4 KJV). When I hear that scripture, I remember the trip to a rundown house in the Kentucky mountains. I remember that Thanksgiving meal of fried bologna and cold grits shared at a card table with Bobby. And, I remember that Thanksgiving is not what is on our table. Thanksgiving is what is in our hearts.

* * * * *

ADVENT

11.

THE MEANING OF ADVENT

A young woman was startled by the news that she was pregnant. She had not had the first inkling, nor had she any reason to believe she was with child. She had saved herself for marriage. The attendant, dressed all in white, was neither a nurse nor a physician. The messenger who broke the news was an angel. The young woman was Mary of Nazareth.

Advent is Mary's time. It is a season of expectancy for the young mother who lives in anticipation. But all of us, men and women alike, share in this pregnancy. This is a time of preparation for the arrival of a child, the Nativity of Jesus. As surely as a young couple makes ready to receive a new child, we, too, must be ready for this new arrival.

When Clare and I got married, we knew that we wanted to have children. We prayed that God would give us a child when the time was right. We became frustrated that God did not meet our schedule. We went for medical help and were told that it was improbable that we would ever have a child biologically. We pondered the possibility of adoption. We were overjoyed when Clare became pregnant but very disappointed when three months later she had a miscarriage. Again we were told that for us the possibility of having children was remote. We began to explore the possibility of adoption more seriously. After several months, Clare was again pregnant. The second pregnancy lasted longer. Our hearts were broken following a second miscarriage. I was angry. Clare was grieving.

On a walk into the woods with clenched fists and gritted teeth, I told God that I did not understand why people around the world were having children like stray cats, yet we could not have a child.

There was no flash of light, no audible voice, but a clear message: "Kirk, how can you expect to be a father until you learn to hurt?"

We initiated the long process of adoption with paperwork, home visits, and medical tests. Within weeks before we were to receive our adopted child, we discovered that Clare was again pregnant. The choice was difficult. Should we terminate adoption and risk another disappointment? Should we continue adoption proceedings with the possibility that we would have two infants just six months apart in age? Our decision to terminate adoption was another grief for us.

Clare carried our child full term. We were expecting our firstborn to arrive on December 18, 1970. As these things often go, the anticipated date came and went, but still no baby.

As Christmas approached, Clare and I waited in Louisville, realizing that we would not be with either of our families for the holidays. We could not travel to New Orleans, where her parents resided, or to Spartanburg, where my family lived. We exchanged gifts with our families by mail.

Christmas Eve arrived; our child had not. We enjoyed dinner together in our home. Before midnight, we opened one gift each. Then we called both families to wish them Merry Christmas.

Just after we went to bed, Clare had her first contraction. Suddenly, we were wide awake! At 5:00 A.M. on Christmas morning, we were on the way to Norton Infirmary in downtown Louisville. A soft, light snow was falling, and the streets were empty as we drove through the dark morning.

At the hospital, I left Clare in labor and delivery and went to admissions to check her in as a patient. When I returned her contractions had stopped, and she was sound asleep. I waited. Then, about noon on Christmas Day she went into hard labor. We had taken Lamaze classes and thought we knew what to expect. In old cowboy movies, when a mother is giving birth, they send the husband out to boil water. Lamaze is something like that. It gives the father a coaching job to do while the mother works very hard.

At 3:26 P.M. on Christmas Day our first child, Michael Kirk Neely, was born. We were overjoyed. Finally, we had a baby, born on Christmas Day! Both sets of grandparents were elated when we telephoned to announce our son's arrival.

The birth of a child is always a miracle.

The word Advent comes from Latin, meaning to come. Some of our carols become prayers of anticipation: "O Come, O Come, Immanuel" and "Come, Thou Long-expected Jesus."

In a spiritual sense, we are all pregnant with anticipation. Every year, we celebrate anew the birth of a child, not just any child, but the Son of God. To hold a newborn in your arms is a reminder of just how precious and fragile a life is. To hold an infant in your arms on Christmas Day is a reminder that in the birth of Jesus, God made himself very vulnerable.

Each Christmas, we draw close to the manger and look into the face of this child. Look closely. Did you notice the resemblance? He is the spitting image of his Father.

"O come let us adore him, Christ the Lord!"

* * * * *

12.

A SEASON OF LIGHT

A motorist was trapped in his automobile on a lonely stretch of a North Dakota highway during a December blizzard. As the snowfall subsided, the traveler ventured out of his car. In the bitterly cold night, he trudged through the drifts toward a faint light in the distance. The light grew brighter as he approached a farmhouse. The home was that of a Jewish family who offered the warmth of hospitality to the stranded man: a chair by the fireplace and a bowl of hot chicken soup. The light that saved the stranger's life came from the glowing candles of a menorah displayed in the window of the farmhouse. A menorah is a candelabra with nine candles used in the celebration of Hanukkah.

Often, Christmas falls within the eight-day observance of Hanukkah. Christians mark the days of Advent by lighting candles in an Advent wreath. They gather for worship in churches on Christmas Eve and Christmas Day. Jewish families mark the days of Hanukkah by lighting candles in a menorah each evening.

The fourth Gospel records an interesting event from the life of Jesus. "Then came the Feast of Dedication at Jerusalem. It was winter and Jesus was in the temple area walking in Solomon's Colonnade" (John 10:22). This passage indicates that Jesus observed Hanukkah, also called the Feast of Dedication or the Festival of Lights.

The origin of Hanukkah dates to 164 B.C.E. when Syria dominated Israel. Antiochus Epiphanes, the king of Syria, was a harsh, cruel tyrant. Jewish worship, including the observance of Passover and the Sabbath, was forbidden under Antiochus. Idols representing Greek gods were set up in the temple, and the scrolls of the Torah were burned. Antiochus slaughtered a pig on the altar of the temple, committing what the Book of Daniel refers to as the abomination of desecration. The Syrians murdered thousands of Jewish dissidents who were steadfastly loyal to their faith.

Three years later, under the leadership of Yehuda the Hammer, better known as Judas Maccabees, the Jews defeated an army of 40,000 Syrians. Judas and his band of four brothers, known by their family name as the Maccabees, liberated Jerusalem. They entered the temple and cleansed it of idols. They also built and dedicated a new altar to replace the one desecrated by Antiochus.

A part of the dedication was the relighting of the eternal flame representing the presence of God in the temple. However, they had only enough consecrated olive oil to keep the light burning for one day. By Jewish law, consecrating new oil would require eight days. Miraculously, the small cruse of oil continued to burn for eight days.

Hanukkah, which means dedication, commemorates this divine blessing. It is an eight-day festival of thanksgiving and rededication for the Jewish community. Jewish families light candles in the menorah each evening. The center taper, known as the servant candle, is used to light the other eight, each in turn as the days pass. By the eighth night all candles are burning.

The scriptures speak of God as "the light in whom there is no darkness" (I John 1:5). For Christians, the celebration of Christmas includes symbols of that heavenly light: the star of Bethlehem and the candles in an Advent wreath. For Jews, the symbols of divine light are the star of David and the candles of the menorah. In this season of light, we recognize and respect both traditions.

In 1973, Clare and I moved our family to Winston-Salem, North Carolina. It was in that good place that we learned about the Moravians. Church historians regard the Moravians as the first Protestants. The denomination originated in Czechoslovakia around 1415. Started by a Catholic priest named John Hus, the movement was established as a reaction against alleged misdeeds within the Roman Catholic Church. Hus wanted to return the practices of the church in Bohemia and Moravia to the purer customs of early Christianity including providing liturgy in the language of the people, allowing lay people to receive communion of both bread and wine, permitting clergy to marry, and eliminating indulgences.

The Hussites, as they were widely known, became a persecuted church until they found refuge on the estate of Count Nikolaus Ludwig von Zinzendorf. They moved across the border from Moravia to Zinzendorf's property, thus giving them the name Moravians. Also known as Bohemian Brethren and United Brothers, the group was the beginning of the Count's vision of a model Christian community. These Christians, called *Unitas Fratrum*, have become a worldwide missionary movement.

The Moravians made their way from Czechoslovakia to Germany to Bethlehem, Pennsylvania. A contingent settled in Salem, North Carolina, on 10,000 acres known as Wachovia. Today many of the area attractions preserve the history of these settlers and educate visitors about their origins and influence. Our family adopted several of the Moravian traditions while we lived in Pfafftown, north of Winston-Salem.

A Moravian star is the very first Christmas decoration to appear at our home. I usually hang it on our front porch the Friday after Thanksgiving where it remains in place until Epiphany. The star is a polyhedron with multiple points. Originating in the Moravian boarding schools in Germany in the nineteenth century as an exercise in geometry, the star proclaims the hope of Advent. The bright white star reminds us of God, who caused the light to shine out of darkness. It represents the star that pointed the way to Bethlehem. From the beginning of Advent until the Day of Epiphany, our Moravian star proclaims, "The light shines in the darkness, and the darkness has not overcome it" (John 1:5).

There are several ways of marking the days during the season. Advent calendars begin on the first of December and count the days until Christmas. These large colorful calendars have twenty-four windows, one for each day of December leading up to Christmas Day. One window is opened every day during Advent. In many of these calendars, each window opens to reveal an image or a portion of the story of the Nativity of Jesus. More elaborate Advent calendars have concealed in each window a small gift, such as a toy or a chocolate candy.

Advent calendars can take other forms. In years past, we have enjoyed a cloth Advent calendar that featured a large green felt tree. Each day a tiny Christmas ornament was pinned to the tree. More recently, we have counted the days with a wooden Advent calendar given to us by my mother. The wooden Christmas tree is adorned with miniature ornaments hung on brass nail pegs one day at a time. Now, our grandchildren delight in hanging the decorations just as much as our children did.

An Advent wreath is another way to mark the approach of Christmas. Four candles are arranged on a table in a circular wreath. Each Sunday during Advent a new candle is lighted. A white Christ candle is in the center. It is lighted on Christmas Day. The meaning of the candles in the wreath can vary from year to year. The five candles may represent Mary, Joseph, the shepherds, the magi, with the center candle representing the Christ Child. The five candles may stand for the promises of Christmas: hope, faith, peace, joy, and love. The candles may represent the roles of Jesus as king, priest, prophet, servant, and savior. Or the candles can correspond to the names of the Messiah from Isaiah: Wonderful Counselor, Mighty God, Everlasting Father, Prince of Peace, and Immanuel.

We enjoy several Advent wreaths in our home. One was made for us by Dr. Bob Cooper, a dear friend and fellow pastor, in his workshop. Constructed from simple wooden blocks, the sturdy wreath is at the center of our breakfast table. Another wreath, handmade by a potter in Seagrove, North Carolina, graces our dining room table. In our foyer is a wreath that we purchased in Old Salem. It features a tiny Moravian star on a dowel at the center and cornhusk Nativity figures.

Saint Lucia Day is observed on December 13. Lucia's name means light. The celebration is associated with Scandinavian countries where winter darkness comes early and stays long. In traditional celebrations, a young woman dressed as Saint Lucia brings light and sweets to her family. The girl wears a wreath of candles as a crown.

Our daughter, Betsy, was given such a crown with battery powered candles by her fairy godmother, a long-time family friend. Betsy enjoyed playing the part of Saint Lucia wearing her glowing diadem, usually serving Moravian sugar cake to our family early on the morning of December 13.

One of the wonderful traditions that we acquired from the Moravians is the Christmas Eve candlelight service. Sometimes called a Moravian love feast, the service features the serving of Moravian coffee and a sweet roll. Each worshiper receives a candle from a server. The beeswax candles, trimmed in fireproof red paper, remind worshipers of the gift of Christ. The traditional Moravian hymn "Morning Star" is sung. This responsive hymn is led by the clear, high voice of a child.

> Morning Star, O cheering sight!
> Ere thou camest how dark earth's night!
> Morning Star, O cheering sight!
> Ere thou camest how dark earth's night!
> Jesus mine, in me shine;
> In me shine, Jesus mine.
> Fill my heart with light divine.
>
> Morning Star, my soul's true light,
> Tarry not, dispel my night.
> Morning Star, my soul's true light,
> Tarry not, dispel my night.
> Jesus mine, in me shine;
> In me shine, Jesus mine.
> Fill my heart with light divine.

Jesus said, "I am ...the bright and morning star" (Revelation 22:16). In the season of Advent, the light of the world is Jesus.

* * * * *

13.

SURVIVING THE CHRISTMAS RUSH

The Christmas rush begins the day after Thanksgiving and continues until after the New Year. Most of us fill our calendars with activities observing the holiday season. Busy schedules and deadlines make us feel pushed and harried. We are constantly reminded of the dwindling number of shopping days until Christmas Day.

A sign announcing the last day to mail packages in order to ensure arrival by Christmas is prominently displayed at the Post Office. Family gatherings and social occasions, heaped on top of our regular responsibilities, leave us irritable and exhausted. Charitable events and faith group activities, though well-intentioned, add to the demands upon our time.

The holidays offer us many rich cultural opportunities. Every town has its own Christmas parade and display of Christmas lights. Musical presentations abound, from Tchaikovsky's *Nutcracker* to Handel's *Messiah*, from school programs to choir cantatas. A difficult reality to grasp is that no matter how we may try, we cannot do everything.

As one weary soul said in late November, "Trying to find a free evening during the holidays is like trying to find a homegrown tomato in my vegetable garden in December."

A major part of seasonal stress for many is increased financial anxiety. The day after Thanksgiving, the busiest shopping day of the year, has been dubbed Black Friday. The first workday following Thanksgiving is now called Cyber Monday, the busiest online shopping day of the year. For many, overspending becomes the norm. Credit card debt spins out of control as buying frenzies escalate and consume us, leaving many to struggle with an avalanche of bills come January.

"I hate Christmas," one beleaguered husband and father said. "Every year my family spends so much that I am barely able to pay off the debt before the next Christmas. Then they do it all over again."

A simple solution is to have a reasonable plan. Our holiday calendar needs to include time for family, personal reflection, and rest and relaxation, as well as activities that are selected, by priority, from our array of options. Our holiday budget needs to allow for giving meaningful gifts to family and friends as well as charitable contributions. Develop a plan that works for you and your family rather than allowing the expenditure of time and money to spin out of control like a renegade helicopter.

The holidays for Jill were always hectic. She operated a catering business from her home. She had numerous parties and receptions on her calendar. There was more to do than she could squeeze into her schedule.

One year she decided to send her Christmas cards early. Jill was the kind of person who kept meticulous records from year to year of cards sent and cards received. She resolved to purge her list, striking from the list the name of any person who had failed to send her a card for the past two years. She purchased the required number of cards and enough holiday stamps to mail them. She added a brief greeting and her signature to each card before mailing them ahead of the postal deadline.

As Christmas approached, Jill received cards in her mail box nearly every day. Much to her chagrin, several of the people she had purged from her extensive list had sent her cards. One busy Friday, while out shopping for Christmas gifts at a stationery store, she picked up a box of twenty-five generic holiday cards. She felt compelled to send a card to every person from whom she had received one. By Christmas Eve, she had mailed all but three of the additional cards to people previously expunged from her list.

A few days after Christmas, as Jill was paying her bills, she reached for one of the leftover generic cards, belatedly remembering that she had not even taken time to read the inside verse before she sent them.

She opened the card and read in dismay: "This little card is just to say, your Christmas gift is on the way." Oops!

Rushing through Christmas can be costly. Not only can we become overextended in time, energy, and money, but we may also become depleted emotionally and spiritually.

Many of our Christmas carols remind us that we need calmness in our souls. Silence, stillness, and peacefulness are important to our most beneficial observance of this season. Finding the quiet center is the way to enjoy the season and preserve our sanity.

The words of John Greenleaf Whittier may become our prayer:

> Dear Lord and Father of mankind,
> Forgive our foolish ways!
> Reclothe us in our rightful mind,
> In purer lives thy service find,
> In deeper reverence praise.

> Drop thy still dews of quietness,
> Till all our strivings cease;
> Take from our souls the strain and stress,
> And let our ordered lives confess
> The beauty of thy peace.

* * * * *

14.

CHRISTMAS CARDS AND LETTERS

In December 1928, just prior to the Great Depression, Mildred King walked into a card shop to look for a Christmas greeting for her brother. Times were hard. There was little she could afford to purchase.

Being British, she was attracted to a card with an illustration of a tartan-clad Scotsman reading by candlelight. The message inside read, "Do not get careless and lose this card. You can send it next year if times get hard. So sign your name in pencil."

For the next fifty years, Mildred King and her brother took turns signing their name and the date in pencil and mailing the card back and forth to each other.

After her brother died, Mildred felt sure that the card must have been discarded. To her surprise, just a few days before Christmas, she opened an envelope and there was the card, signed and dated in pencil by her nephew. The tradition continued into the next generation.

At our home Christmas cards start appearing in our mail the day after Thanksgiving. We receive them until well after the New Year. These greetings from family and friends far and near are welcomed blessings in our home. When our children return home for Christmas, they enjoy looking through the cards, especially the ones that have family pictures and personal notes. Many of the photos find a place on our refrigerator.

The tradition of exchanging Christmas cards began in the 1840s when Queen Victoria sent cards from her palace. Within three years, commercial Christmas cards had been introduced throughout England.

The first commercial Christmas cards, commissioned by Sir Henry Cole in London in 1843, featured an illustration by John Callcott Horsley. In 1875, Louis Prang introduced Victorian-style cards in the United States. The first official White House card was sent in 1953 by President Eisenhower.

Many charitable organizations offer special Christmas cards as a fundraising tool. The most famous are those produced by the United

Nations Children's Fund (UNICEF). The wonderful tradition of UNICEF Christmas cards began in 1949.

From the beginning, Christmas cards have been avidly collected. Queen Mary amassed a large collection that is now housed in the British Museum. Specimens from the golden age of printing (1840s-1890s) are especially prized and bring in large sums at auctions. In December 2005, one of Horsley's original cards sold for nearly $18,000.

Each year Clare and I order Christmas and Hanukkah postage stamps to use on our holiday mailings. Many countries produce brightly colored official Christmas stamps. They usually depict some aspect of the Christmas tradition or a Nativity scene. These holiday stamps have also become collectables. In 2004, the German Post Office gave away 20 million free scented stickers to make Christmas cards smell either like a fir Christmas tree, cinnamon, gingerbread, honey-wax candles, baked apples, or oranges. I wonder if postal workers enjoyed those mingled aromas as they processed the mail.

Advances in digital photography and printing have provided the technology for people to craft their own cards. These computer-designed cards may include personal touches such as family photos and holiday snapshots.

Many people send cards to both close friends and distant acquaintances, potentially making the sending of cards a labor-intensive chore. The greeting inside the card can be a brief personal note.

In recent years, technology has led to the decline of the Christmas card. E-mail and Facebook allow for more frequent contact with friends and family. Those in the younger generation, raised without handwritten correspondence, find addressing cards tedious. Web sites now offer free online Christmas cards. Even Hallmark provides e-cards.

Some people take the annual mass mailing of cards as an opportunity to update everybody with their latest family news. They may include a Christmas letter reporting on the year's events. I almost never read these lengthy epistles, but Clare reads them and points out details I should know.

Christmas letters meet with a mixed reception. Family members may object to how the family Christmas letter presents them. An entire episode of the popular television show "Everybody Loves Raymond" was built around conflict over the content of just such a letter.

Friends sent this parody of a Christmas letter to us. I include it because it is funny. The names have been changed to protect the guilty.

Dear Friends,
This has truly been another year of magic and wonder.
Kelly, almost 3, continues to amaze the professors at Harvard University with her aptitude in foreign languages. She intends to spend this holiday translating *War and Peace* into Arabic and Cantonese.

Ernest, now 5, is growing by leaps and bounds. After he got his first set of building blocks he seemed quite interested in large buildings. This year he designed his first skyscraper, and ground was broken in Hong Kong for the new Ernest McKnight Towers.

Janet had a busy year. Along with her work as President of the American Cancer Society, she has introduced a series of children's novels and a line of handmade active-wear. We are particularly proud of Mom. She is a starting forward on the United States World Cup Soccer Team.

Dan was immersed in his graduate school studies and accepted a Nobel Prize for his discoveries in quantum physics. We are proud of his work serving on the Board of Directors of IBM, Coca-Cola, and Walt Disney.

We were able to squeeze a little traveling in this year. We started in Aspen, went to Belarus, the Congo, Denmark, Ethiopia, the Falkland Islands, Greenland, Holland, Italy, Japan, Malaysia, New Zealand, South Korea, Venezuela, and Zaire. Our trip sailing the new boat around the world was a great experience for the kids.

Other than that, it was a very quiet year. So from our household to yours, all the blessings of the season and may your New Year be prosperous.

The McKnight Family,
Janet, Dan, Ernest, and Kelly
P.S. Yesterday we won the $150 Million Powerball Lottery.

It is a funny letter, but it misses the point of a Christmas greeting.

What is the purpose of a greeting card or a holiday letter? I have often thought that the fruit of the spirit delineated by the Apostle Paul in his letter to the Galatians would make a reliable guide for designing Christmas greetings. "The fruit of the Spirit is love, joy, peace, forbearance, kindness, goodness, faithfulness, gentleness, and self-control" (Galatians 5:22-23).

Most of the virtues listed by the Apostle Paul as the fruit of the Spirit would make a lovely Christmas card, except for the last one. "May God grant you love, joy, and peace at Christmas," would be well-received. But, imagine receiving a beautiful holiday card with the message, "Our prayer is that God will grant you self-control during the holidays."

Come to think of it, that might be exactly what many of us need to hear.

❖ ❖ ❖ ❖ ❖

15.

THE CHRISTMAS ROSE

According to legend, when the magi presented their extravagant offerings of myrrh, frankincense, and gold to the Christ Child, a peasant girl stood outside the door quietly weeping.

She, too, had sought the Christ Child. She desired to bring him a gift, but she had nothing to offer because she was poor. She had searched the countryside for one small flower to bring him. The winter had been cold. She could not find even a single bloom to offer as a gift.

As she stood there crying, an angel passing by saw her sorrow. Stooping down, he brushed aside the snow at her feet. And there sprang up a cluster of beautiful winter roses, waxen white with pink tipped petals.

"Neither myrrh, nor frankincense, nor gold," said the angel, "is more fitting for the Christ Child than these pure Christmas roses."

Joyfully, the girl gathered the flowers and made them her offering to the Holy Child.

Flowers at Christmas are not so uncommon here in the Upstate of South Carolina. As Christmas approaches, camellia blossoms and a few David Austin roses are usually blooming in my garden. On our front porch, red geraniums still offer a display suitable for the Advent season.

The Christmas cactus, also known as orchid cactus, is an easily grown favorite of the holidays. Its pendulous stems make a dramatic display. In our home we have several grouped together. Most of our plants were cultivated from a single plant given to us following the death of our son Erik. For us, the Christmas cactus is an enduring symbol of hope.

The Christmas rose, also known as the snow rose or winter rose, blooms during the winter in the mountains of central Europe. Most horticulturists agree that the true Christmas rose is *hellebores*. It is called the Christmas rose more for its rose-like flowers than for the reliability of seeing it bloom at Christmas time. A low-growing vigorous evergreen, it can bloom anytime from December to April, depending on conditions. The prolific flowers are usually white, with green-tinged centers that age to pink. In the South, *hellebores* is more commonly known as the Lenten rose because it usually blooms after the first of the year.

The very first Christmas gift we received last year was a magnificent red poinsettia, sometimes called the Christmas star or the winter rose. It is a subtropical plant native to Mexico and Central America.

The ancient Aztecs prized the poinsettia as a symbol of purity. Mexico's early Christians adopted poinsettias as Christmas flowers. In both Central and North America, the plant is used as a Christmas decoration.

The poinsettia has a South Carolina connection. The plant made its debut in the United States due to the efforts of a South Carolina statesman. Joel Poinsett represented South Carolina in the United States Congress from 1821 to 1826. He was appointed the first American Ambassador to Mexico in 1825. During this time, he visited southern Mexico, discovering the plant which was later named for him.

A bright red poinsettia usually graces our dining room table during the holidays. The poinsettia has sometimes been called a Christmas rose.

From diverse cultures come many variations on the legend of the Christmas rose. A Mexican legend explains that a little girl who could not afford a gift for the Christ Child picked weeds along the roadsides. A priest told her that a simple gift, presented in love, was acceptable in God's eyes. As she brought the weeds into the church, they blossomed into red flowers – hence, the miracle of the poinsettia.

Whether your favorite Christmas flower is *hellebores*, poinsettia, Christmas cactus, or a geranium protected on the front porch, their beauty brings added joy to a season usually associated with snow and ice.

Flowers that appear at Christmas are sometimes quite surprising. Recently, even after several killing frosts, I saw a knockout rose bush covered with reddish pink blossoms. The plant thrives in a protected area next to a south-facing wall. Surely, it, too, could be regarded as a Christmas rose.

The words to an old fifteenth-century Christmas carol, originally written in German and translated into English, came to mind. The lyrics suggest that the Christmas rose symbolizes, for Christians, the true meaning of the season.

> Lo, how a rose e'er blooming from tender stem hath sprung!
> Of Jesse's lineage coming, as men of old have sung.
> It came, a floweret bright, amid the cold of winter,
> When half spent was the night.

A first-grader with a pink ribbon in her hair came to my office after Sunday School on the second Sunday of Advent. She carried a jelly jar filled with a bouquet of pansies picked from her mother's flowerbed.

"Dr. Kirk, I brought you a Christmas present!" she said excitedly.

I bent down on one knee to accept the glass container filled with bright-faced purple, yellow, and white pansies. She gave me a big hug and exclaimed, "Merry Christmas!"

I put the makeshift vase on my desk.

After the worship service, I admired the gift. Those flowers plucked from the garden by a child's tiny hands looked for all the world like Christmas roses to me.

* * * * *

16.
O TANNENBAUM

Last year, as in every past year, I hoisted from its stand the Christmas tree that had graced our home for several weeks. As always, I wrestled it out of the front door, leaving an impressive accumulation of Fraser fir needles in its wake. Returning to the living room, I found Clare already vacuuming the pesky remains from the carpet.

I raised, yet again, the obvious question, first uttered by Uncle Asbury, long ago, standing in the same room in the same house, "Who ever thought that cutting a tree, carrying it inside the house, and letting it dry out for a few weeks was a good idea?"

Legend has it that one cold starlit night just before Christmas, Martin Luther brought a fir tree into his home, decorating it with candles to bring the light of Christmas inside. Unfortunately, a home with a freshly cut tree inside may offer more than just the light of Christmas.

Our good friends in the pest control business have numerous stories about unwanted critters nestled in Christmas trees that gain entrance into homes. A praying mantis egg case lodged deep within the branches may breach a home undetected. Warmed to room temperature, the eggs will hatch, releasing hundreds of green insects. Similar experiences with ladybug beetles are not uncommon. While both the praying mantis and the ladybug beetle are useful insects in the great outdoors, they are regarded as intruders when they come indoors.

When I was a boy, my dad and I cut our Christmas trees from the family farm in southern Spartanburg County. On a Saturday afternoon several weeks before Christmas, my dad and granddad, along with uncles and cousins, scoured the woods. We gathered holly branches laden with red berries and shot mistletoe loaded with white berries out of the tops of oak trees. With a bow saw, we cut a red cedar Christmas tree for each family home. We loaded the greenery onto the bed of a three-ton lumber truck and made our way back to Spartanburg.

On one occasion, my dad, my brothers, and I carried a fragrant red cedar into our living room. The family decorated the tree that night, enjoying popcorn and hot chocolate. Several days later, Mama, in a panic, telephoned Dad at the lumberyard. It was highly unusual for my mother to call the lumberyard and even more out of the ordinary for my dad to leave his place of business. But, he rushed home to haul the red cedar, decorations and all, into the front yard. Our Christmas tree was crawling with red spiders. After spraying it with foul-smelling pesticide, he later brought the cedar back into the house. That Christmas, the cedar fragrance never returned, even after we hung cedar-scented car deodorizers like Christmas ornaments on the branches.

In recent years, Clare and I have purchased Fraser firs for our Christmas tree. Last year, I noticed that our North Carolina-grown fir had a tag attached to the top, indicating that the tree had been treated with pesticides. It was certified to be insect free, but that comforting assurance was short-lived. Within several days, creepy black bugs appeared all over the carpet and the drapes near the tree. The certified fir was infested with black pine aphids. Our aforementioned pest control friends rushed to the rescue, thoroughly spraying the tree and our living room.

When our family was young, we spread out an old quilt, making a pallet beneath the tree. The children pretended to be camping in the woods. As a little boy our son Erik often slept under the Christmas tree.

When Erik died in November 2000, figuring out how to celebrate Christmas without him was daunting. A month after his death, on a cold December day, Clare suggested that we place a Christmas tree on his grave. We've adopted the custom and put a tree next to Erik's marker each year. We add a simple brass star on top. Throughout the season cousins and others unknown to us add a few ornaments. The thought of our son sleeping under a Fraser fir is comforting.

We enjoy the beauty and the fragrance of a fresh Christmas tree in our living room, even though we may have to endure an occasional invasion of insects and the inevitable removal of dried needles.

Perhaps the most beautiful Christmas tree of all is the one we place each year at Greenlawn Cemetery on Erik's grave. When I visit his grave and see Erik's tree, the last line of a beloved Christmas carol, like a lullaby, comes to mind.

"Sleep in heavenly peace. Sleep in heavenly peace."

* * * * *

17.
THE JOY OF STORIES

The season of Advent presents many challenges to a pastor. Here are two.

The first is to tell the old, old story to people who have heard it over and over again as well as to those for whom it is only vaguely familiar. The preaching task is to retain and restore the mystery and wonder of the original story. We have the responsibility of liberating Mary and Joseph, the shepherds and the magi from confinement as stained glass icons, freeing them to be real people again.

The second challenge is to remember that Christmas is a time of sharp emotional contrasts. Many people are happy and have little difficulty finding joy in the season, but December brings sadness to others. For those who are hurting, the coming of Christmas may be filled with dread, despair, bitterness, and anger. Some are freshly wounded; others carry deep scars from years gone by. For them, Christmas is anything but the season to be jolly. They suffer while others celebrate.

In forty-five years of pastoral ministry, I have learned that there is no better way to present the message of hope and love that is at the heart of Christmas than through stories that parallel and perhaps merge with the original story.

My first year as pastor at Morningside Baptist Church, I told a Christmas story as a part of the sermon on the last Sunday of Advent. I recounted the time I played the part of Joseph in a children's Christmas play at Croft Baptist Church. The story of that pageant is included in this book as Chapter 25, "Christmas at Croft."

The Morningside congregation was delighted with the change in format. Several friends encouraged me to present a new story every Christmas. In subsequent years, on the Sunday a week or so before December 25, we remove the pulpit from the sanctuary. It is replaced with an easy chair where I sit to tell an original Christmas story, written as a gift to the congregation. Nine of those stories are collected in the book *Comfort and Joy*, published in 2005 by Hub City Writers Project.

Our family enjoys a good tale. The holiday season is a time for good stories. Whether read in a book, viewed as a television special, or seen as a movie, Christmas stories abound. From *Frosty the Snowman* to *It's a*

Wonderful Life, a good story lifts the spirits. *Miracle on 34th Street* and *A Christmas Carol* are worth viewing or reading again and again. *How the Grinch Stole Christmas* is a part of every Christmas for us.

Let me share a story behind a story.

In 1823, Clement C. Moore wrote his famous poem, "A Visit from St. Nicholas." He described St. Nick's sleigh being pulled by flying reindeer. While reindeer only fly in fantasy, they have been a useful means of transportation in the most northern parts of the world for centuries.

In the past, wild reindeer ranged in northernmost countries around the globe. In North America they are called caribou. They roamed throughout Canada, Alaska, and the northern continental United States. These wild herds have disappeared, though some populations can still be found.

Even now reindeer are not fully domesticated. They graze free on pasture grounds. They are raised for their meat, hides, milk, and antlers. The animals are also used for transportation.

During the spring migration, small herds group together. Reindeer travel further than any other terrestrial mammal. They will walk more than 3,000 miles in a year, traveling nearly thirty miles a day. Reindeer can swim with ease. They will not hesitate to swim across a large lake or broad river. You can almost believe that they could fly!

Gene Autry, the singing cowboy, crooned, "You know Dasher and Dancer, Prancer and Vixen, Comet and Cupid, Donder and Blitzen." The names are from Clement Moore's poem. Donder and Blitzen are the German words for thunder and lightning.

Autry sang a question: "But do you recall the most famous reindeer of all?" Rudolph is, of course, the answer. But there are other reindeer characters that have been named in animated films: Olive, actually a dog who believes that she's a reindeer; Fireball, a yearling buck who befriends Rudolph before the start of the reindeer games; and Clarice, a yearling doe who thinks Rudolph is cute.

Rudolph, in fact, is the most famous reindeer of all. He has a remarkable and a disputed story. One version is attributed to the book *Stories behind the Best-Loved Songs of Christmas* by Ace Collins. According to the Collins version, the story of Rudolph was written by a grieving and depressed father trying to bring comfort to his little daughter while her mother was dying of cancer. The account has been especially meaningful for people who are having a difficult time during the holidays.

Paul Harvey shared a different account in one of his *The Rest of the Story* radio segments. According to Harvey, Bob May worked as a copywriter for the Montgomery Ward Company. His boss asked him to write a children's story for a Christmas promotion. Bob took elements from his own life and from "The Ugly Duckling" by Hans Christian Andersen.

As a child, Bob was small for his age. He had been bullied by other boys. He was often called names by his schoolmates who thought he was too short to compete in sports.

May's four-year-old daughter, Barbara, was recruited to help develop the story to make sure Rudolph would appeal to children. Bob read his lines to Barbara. If she did not understand the meaning of any of the words, he would simplify the vocabulary.

May pitched his story to Montgomery Ward executives. The company turned down the first proposal and asked Bob to return with a second draft. When May came back, his improved story included sketches by an illustrator from the company. The story was approved.

The company distributed 2,400,000 copies of the book *Rudolph the Red-Nosed Reindeer* during the 1939 and 1940 Christmas season promotions. By 1946, Montgomery Ward had printed and distributed more than six million copies of *Rudolph*. That year the company enjoyed financial success. The executives awarded Bob May the copyright to his popular Christmas story. The book became a bestseller. Toys and marketing deals followed. Bob May became wealthy from the story he had created.

Bob's brother-in-law, Johnny Marks, wrote a song adaptation of *Rudolph the Red-Nosed Reindeer*. Bing Crosby and Dinah Shore both turned down the opportunity to record the song. Instead, Gene Autry recorded it. "Rudolph the Red-Nosed Reindeer," released in 1949, became a phenomenal success. It is still loved today.

Could I encourage you to share a good story with someone you love this Christmas? Nothing comes to mind? Begin with the Gospel of Luke Chapter 2. There you will find a good adventure story that is the source of all Christmas stories.

* * * * *

18.
CHRISTMAS CAROLS IN THE DARK

Mr. E. P. Todd was the principal of Cooperative Elementary School for many years. I, along with all seven of my brothers and sisters, were students at the school while Mr. Todd was the man in charge. He was a kind man with a tender heart and a firm hand. Mr. Todd was loved by pupils, parents, and teachers alike.

After his retirement, this remarkable man, who had made such an impact on so many children, lived into his nineties. One Christmas, after my siblings and I were all married adults with children of our own, we learned that Mr. Todd's wife was seriously ill. After our Neely Family Christmas Eve gathering, Dad suggested that we all go caroling at the Todd home. Without hesitation we piled into vans and minivans for the opportunity. The night air was cold as we gathered in the carport outside Mr. Todd's home. We sang one carol after another. Mr. and Mrs. Todd came to the backdoor. She was in a wheelchair. He opened the door and smiled with tears running down his cheeks.

When we finished the last carol, Mr. Todd passed peppermints around until he ran out. "You have made our Christmas," he said. The experience certainly helped to make ours.

Saint Francis of Assisi is credited with originating the custom of outdoor caroling. He would gather a group of singers and move through the streets lifting the songs of Christmas.

Indoors or out carols are important parts of the celebration. For example, at King's College Chapel in Cambridge, England, the Christmas Eve service is a Festival of Nine Lessons and Carols. The Festival was introduced in 1918 to bring a more imaginative approach to worship. It was first broadcast on radio in 1928. Now it is heard by millions of people around the world. The service includes carols and readings from the Bible. The opening carol is always "Once in Royal David's City." The first verse is always sung *a cappella* by a young choirboy.

As Christmas approaches, the sounds of carols fill the air. Not only can the music celebrating the birth of Christ be heard in churches and cathedrals, but it can also be recognized in the background at shopping malls, used car lots, and restaurants. Television commercials and the radio play the familiar songs of the season.

Much of the music of the holidays projects the happy attitude, "'tis the season to be jolly." In the grocery store I have heard the late Burl Ives encouraging shoppers, "Have a holly, jolly Christmas."

For many people, like Mr. and Mrs. Todd, the Christmas season is anything but jolly. Each Christmas, Holly Irvin, the Minister of Music with whom I currently serve, encourages church members to go Christmas caroling to those in the church who have been recently bereaved. One Sunday just before Christmas, in the midst of a gathering recession, five men, all married with children, told me they had lost their jobs that very week. Four of those five unemployed men went caroling with their families. Caroling is a significant ministry for the singers and for the hearers.

A woman who lives alone suffers severe bouts of depression and anxiety, especially at this time of year. She told me recently that sometimes at night, the whole world seems so dark. When she starts having heart palpitations, she sings Christmas carols. She told me, "I especially love the line, 'a thrill of hope, the weary world rejoices.' Just singing carols seems to help."

The events surrounding the first Christmas were hardly reason to be jolly. A young teenage woman traveling by donkey found shelter in a stable where she gave birth to her child. A carpenter was called upon to serve as a midwife for the woman he loved. Shepherds were minding their own business on a hillside near Bethlehem when all heaven broke loose. They were terrified. Then, angels sang the first Christmas carol, "Glory to God in the Highest!"

On Christmas Day 2007, the Associated Press published the story of Bud Marquis. Bud, then 79 years old, lived near Homestead, Florida. The news story reminded readers that Bud was a forgotten hero. On December 29, 1972, Eastern Airlines Flight 401 was preparing to land at the Miami International Airport. Just after 11:30 P.M., following an uneventful flight from New York, the jet carrying 163 passengers and thirteen crew members began its approach.

The light on the control panel that indicates whether the plane's nose gear is down had not yet illuminated. The pilot informed the control tower they would have to circle while crew members solved the problem. Air traffic controllers gave their permission. The crew was instructed to maintain an altitude of 2,000 feet.

The pilot thought he had engaged the autopilot. He had not. Instead Flight 401 went into a slow descent.

About twenty miles west of the airport, the crew received permission to turn back and make another approach. It was then that the pilot realized that the big jet was just a few feet above the Everglades. Seven seconds later, the plane's left wing dug into the swamp going 227 miles per hour, sending it spinning like a pinwheel.

On that moonless night, Marquis was gigging frogs from his airboat. The city of Miami was just a distant pinpoint of light. From ten miles away, Marquis saw a fiery orange flash.

Bud Marquis had served for years as a state game officer. He knew how to pick out island silhouettes in the dark and how to feel the changing terrain beneath his boat. Speeding across the saw grass and mud, the airboat reached a levee where Bud thought he'd seen the flash.

When he cut his engine, he heard a voice crying out, "I can't hold my head up anymore!"

Jet fuel seeped into his boots when he jumped into the water to pull the man up. He could see passengers still strapped in their seats, some turned facedown in the water.

In the alligator-infested swamp, a flight attendant gathered survivors around her. When they heard the airboat, they started singing Christmas carols so rescuers could find them. Bud heard the carolers and headed toward the singing.

Using a flashlight, Marquis motioned helicopters hovering above the wreckage toward a nearby levee.

On that dark December night, Bud Marquis pulled survivors from the water, taking a few at a time to the levee. He ferried arriving rescuers in to the wreckage site.

Ninety-four passengers, three pilots, and two flight attendants were dead. Investigators marveled that anyone had survived. In all, seventy-seven people were rescued, many of them by Bud Marquis.

For Marquis, the events of that night so long ago were vividly etched in his mind. He would always remember the sound of carols that dark night in the swamp.

Many folks have memories of a dark Christmas. After our son Erik died, that year was a difficult time for our family. We simplified our celebration, not decorating as extensively as we had in the past. A fresh wreath with a red bow on the front door and a stately Fraser fir tree in the living room reminded us of the beauty of the season. Our Nativity scenes and Advent wreaths reminded us of the meaning of the season. But it was the music that carried us along, bringing comfort and joy to our souls.

We celebrated Christmas Eve with my larger family at my parents' home. Little did we know that my mother was spending her last Christmas with us before her death the following April. On Christmas night, Clare prepared dinner for our family. We invited Mama and Dad to join us.

After a delicious meal, dessert, and coffee, I heard a knock at our front door. When I answered, I was surprised to see my good friend and colleague Ron Wells. We had served together on a church staff in times past. He was a remarkable Minister of Music. At the time, Ron was in a battle for his life against cancer. Yet, there he was at our front door, seated in a wheelchair, and surrounded by his wife, children, and grandchildren. The moment I opened the door, they started singing. Our family gathered on the front porch that cold Christmas night to listen to the carols. Tears came to my eyes just as tears had come to Mr. Todd's on a Christmas years before.

The carols of Christmas bring hope and healing to broken hearts and troubled souls.

Phillips Brooks wrote, "Yet in thy dark streets shineth, the everlasting light. The hopes and fears of all the years are met in thee tonight."

From Bethlehem to the Everglades, hope and fear still meet in the dark places of our lives. The deep longing for hope is reason enough to sing.

* * * * *

19.

THE PRINCE OF PEACE

Clare and I have dear friends who traveled to Italy for their Christmas holiday in December 2002. Our friends spent nearly a week in the city of Rome. As most tourists do, they visited a number of beautiful historic churches and cathedrals. At Christmastime, every church in Rome displays a Nativity scene. Italy is the country in which St. Francis of Assisi originated the custom of the Nativity scene.

Our friends took pictures of many of these manger scenes that present in miniature the birth of Christ. As those photographs revealed, the birth of Jesus can be depicted in various ways. Some of the Nativity scenes are the artistic work of skilled craftsmen who retell the story of Advent with exquisite artistry. Some are delicate woodcarvings; others are sculpted from Italian marble. Some of the manger scenes are tasteful and pleasing; others are garish and excessive. A few of the Nativity scenes are downright shocking.

At a church named San Clemente, a manger scene included the simple figures of Mary, Joseph, and the baby Jesus. The Holy Family was surrounded by concertina wire, a razor-like barbed wire. Instead of shepherds and wise men, sheep and camels, implements of war surrounded the manger. Tanks and artillery pieces were positioned so that they seemed to aim directly at Jesus. The symbolism of the scene would have been apparent even without the crude sign posted against the wire fence:

CONTRO OGNI GUERRA

The English translation of this eloquent Italian message is,

AGAINST ALL WAR

The image of weapons of war aimed at the infant Jesus is startling and horrifying. Whether he is in the manger with rifles pointed at him or on the cross suffering excruciating agony, the idea of violence against Jesus is repugnant. Yet it was into a world of hatred that Jesus was born. The atrocity of Herod's infanticide against the children of Bethlehem was intended to kill Jesus (Matthew 2:16). The wanton murder of innocents is unthinkable. From his birth to his death, Jesus proclaimed a message of love in the midst of a world filled with violence.

The cross stands as a symbol of love in a world of hatred. It really does not matter how Jesus died. He could have been put to death by lethal injection, in the electric chair, or before a firing squad. He could have died in a Nazi gas chamber, in a drive-by shooting, or in the Inquisition. The Christian faith affirms that he was born into this world as a supreme gift of divine love to offer his life for our salvation. His birth and death are an act of love for the whole world. When we emulate his love, we become agents of his peace.

The prophet of old declared, "For unto us a child is born, unto us a son is given...And his name shall be called...The Prince of Peace" (Isaiah 9:6 KJV). When Jesus was born, the angels sang, "on earth peace, goodwill toward men!" (Luke 2:14 NKJV). Jesus promised, "Peace I leave with you; my peace I give you. I do not give to you as the world gives. Do not let your hearts be troubled and do not be afraid." (John 14:27). As we prepare to celebrate his birth, our petition is the prayer of St. Francis:

> Lord, make me an instrument of your peace.
> Where there is hatred, let me sow love;
> Where there is injury, pardon;
> Where there is doubt, faith;
> Where there is despair, hope;
> Where there is darkness, light;
> And where there is sadness, joy.
>
> O divine Master, grant that I may not so much seek
> To be consoled as to console;
> To be understood as to understand;
> To be loved as to love.
> For it is in giving that we receive;
> It is in pardoning that we are pardoned;
> And it is in dying that we are born to eternal life.
> Amen.

*****

20.
THE PROMISE OF PEACE

When our children were young, we displayed a wreath on a table in our foyer. We had purchased the decoration when we lived in Winston-Salem, North Carolina. It was a simple circle with four red candles around the perimeter. A tall dowel wrapped in red ribbon lifted a tiny paper Moravian star above a manger scene created entirely out of cornhusk doll figures.

Each Sunday in Advent we gathered our five children around the wreath to light the appropriate candle. One year, on the third Sunday of Advent, we lit the peace candle. After reading a scripture passage from Isaiah about the promise of peace, we sang a Christmas carol.

As I was offering the closing prayer, there shone a great light! Our Advent wreath with cornhusk figures was on fire!

Holy smoke!

I grabbed the flaming wreath and started to dash toward the front door. Clare shouted, "Throw it in the bathtub!"

I stopped in my tracks, turned on my heels, and detoured to the guest bathroom just across the hall. I jerked back the shower curtain, dropped the wreath into the tub, turned on the faucet, and doused the flames with water.

The smoke alarm was blasting. Younger children were crying. Older ones were laughing. All of us were greatly relieved.

Some of the cornhusk figures were burned to a crisp. A few were charred but still recognizable.

To this day, we display a wreath with the manger scene of cornhusk figures. Some of them are replacements, and others are scorched survivors of the fire. I have reworked the wreath. The paper Moravian star has been replaced. We still have candles on the wreath, but, for obvious reasons, we never light them. The figures singed in the fire are a reminder of God's protection.

The wisdom of a Chinese proverb offers sound advice for this season of light. "Better to light a candle than to curse the darkness." True, but please, be careful with those candles!

For many people Christmas can be a very difficult time. Like the figures in our manger scene that were burned on that Advent Sunday, many bear the scars of Christmas past. Those who have carried the burden of grief during the holidays or those who have spent Christmas in the hospital know all too well how difficult this season can be. Some have spent Christmas in prison while others have spent the holidays away from home in military service.

My good friends Leroy and Bonnie Wilson were married for sixty-four years. When asked how long he served in the military during World War II, Leroy answered, "I had to be away from Bonnie for three Christmases."

It was in a world just like this one that Mary and Joseph traveled to Bethlehem. It was into this kind of hardship that Jesus was born, out back, in less than ideal circumstances.

Several of our best-loved carols reflect this truth. Knowing the circumstances behind the creation of some of these songs, the story of the lives and times of the people who wrote them, can lead to a greater appreciation of the music so integral to Christmas.

Recent years have marked a difficult period for many American citizens. The last several Advent seasons have been times of economic hardship, the constant threat of terrorist attacks, and wars that brought pain and sorrow. An oil spill along the Gulf Coast brought pollution and devastation to a region still trying to recover from Hurricane Katrina. More recently, the region has suffered the effects of deadly tornadoes and record flooding.

Our country has seen trying times before, perhaps none more troubling than during the Civil War. It was in the depths of that brutal conflict that Henry Wadsworth Longfellow, one of America's most famous poets, wrote the words to a familiar Christmas carol.

In 1843, Longfellow, already a widower, married Frances Appleton. They settled in Cambridge, Massachusetts. Henry and Fanny eventually had six children. They were a happy family.

The Civil War abruptly destroyed their serenity. It violently interrupted the lives of thousands, North and South.

In the summer of 1861, Fanny Longfellow was melting sealing wax on an envelope when the long folds of her dress caught fire. Her dress ablaze, she ran into Henry's study. Desperately trying to smother the flames with a small rug and his own body, Henry was badly burned on his face, arms, and hands. Fanny's burns were much more severe. She died the next morning.

Longfellow was despondent after his wife's death. Enduring Christmas without Fanny, Henry captured in his journal the sentiments so many have felt through the ages: "How inexpressibly sad are all holidays."

In early December 1863, Henry received word that his oldest son, Charles, a lieutenant in the Army of the Potomac, had been severely wounded. Although Charles would survive, his recovery at that time was uncertain.

Longfellow greeted Christmas with a heavy heart that year. He had lost his wife, his son had nearly died, and the country continued waging war on itself.

The bells that Henry heard ringing that Christmas inspired him to write the poem that would eventually become the carol "I Heard the Bells on Christmas Day."

Longfellow's personal difficulties and the atrocities of war give the words to the carol a deeper meaning.

> I heard the bells on Christmas day
> Their old familiar carols play,
> And wild and sweet the words repeat
> Of peace on earth, good will to men.

> I thought as now this day had come,
> The belfries of all Christendom
> Had rolled along the unbroken song
> Of peace on earth, good will to men.

The third verse takes on a much darker tone, reflecting Longfellow's despondent mood.

> And in despair I bowed my head:
> "There is no peace on earth," I said,
> "For hate is strong and mocks the song
> Of peace on earth, good will to men."

Even in his despair, the fourth verse of the carol offers reason for hope.

> Then pealed the bells more loud and deep;
> "God is not dead, nor doth He sleep;
> The wrong shall fail, the right prevail
> With peace on earth, good will to men."

During Advent, the scorched figures on our wreath and the words to Longfellow's carol will be for me a reminder of one of the most important themes of Christmas. Peace is not the absence of conflict or difficulty. Peace is a gift of grace to the human soul.

* * * * *

CHRISTMAS

21.
KEEPING CHRISTMAS

A church member asked, "What does keeping Christmas mean?"

I learned from internet research that the phrase, keeping Christmas, goes back at least to medieval times. It was certainly used in the Victorian era. Charles Dickens expressed the concept in the conclusion of his story *A Christmas Carol*: "…and it was always said of him [Ebenezer Scrooge], that he knew how to keep Christmas well, if any man alive possessed the knowledge. May that be truly said of us, and all of us! And so, as Tiny Tim observed, God bless us, every one!"

My mother was adopted. In her new family, she had one older sister, whom she called Sister. It was only natural that my seven siblings and I should call this dear woman Aunt Sister. She was a proper Southern lady. Her heritage went back to a plantation in Darlington County. She was the first person I knew who used the expression keeping Christmas.

When the question was raised about the phrase, my thoughts went back to Aunt Sister. What did she mean by keeping Christmas?

Keeping Christmas well means to worship, not only in a cantata or candlelight service, but also with acts of kindness. Even beyond good food, festive decorations, gift-giving, and family time, it is important to keep Christmas in our hearts.

This was a lesson Ebenezer Scrooge had to learn in *A Christmas Carol*. Scrooge had become so self-centered that his life focused solely on material wealth. He refused to light a coal fire, preferring instead to curse the cold weather as he tried to save one more shilling.

Ebenezer had a spiritual ailment. He saw the world around him as a miserable place. The real problem was within his own soul. His malady was the same as the one that afflicted the Grinch.

Dr. Seuss diagnosed the illness in his book *How the Grinch Stole Christmas*.

> The Grinch *hated* Christmas! The whole Christmas season!
> Now, please don't ask why. No one quite knows the reason.
> It *could* be his head wasn't screwed on just right.
> It *could* be, perhaps, that his shoes were too tight.
> But I think that the most likely reason of all

May have been that his heart was two sizes too small.
(Theodor Seuss Geisel, *How The Grinch Stole Christmas*, Random House, New York, 1957)

Both Ebenezer and the Grinch had a diminished heart.

The failures and disappointments of the past made Ebenezer a greedy recluse, uncaring and cruel to the people around him. He had no friends. As Dickens' story unfolds, Scrooge was confronted with the painful truth of his own life. Allowed to glimpse into the future, he came to see himself as a man impoverished in spirit.

The ghosts of Christmas past, present, and future confronted Scrooge with his own spiritual poverty. Through these revelations he decided to change. Much to the astonishment of Bob Cratchit and Tiny Tim, Ebenezer Scrooge became a different man. Though the streets of London were the same, and Tiny Tim still had his affliction, the heart of Ebenezer Scrooge was transformed.

Keeping Christmas requires a change of heart.

One Christmas Aunt Sister sent me the poem "Keeping Christmas," by Henry Van Dyke. Here is a portion of the poem.

There is a better thing than the observance of Christmas Day, and that is, keeping Christmas. Are you willing
- to forget what you have done for other people, and to remember what other people have done for you;
- to ignore what the world owes you, and to think what you owe the world;
- to see that men and women are just as real as you are, and try to look behind their faces to their hearts, hungry for joy;
- to close your book of complaints against the management of the universe, and look around you for a place where you can sow a few seeds of happiness?

Are you willing to do these things even for a day? Then you can keep Christmas.

Are you willing
- to stoop down and consider the needs and desires of little children;
- to remember the weakness and loneliness of people growing old;
- to stop asking how much your friends love you, and ask yourself whether you love them enough;
- to bear in mind the things that other people have to bear in their hearts;

- to try to understand what those who live in the same home with you really want, without waiting for them to tell you;
- to trim your lamp so that it will give more light and less smoke;
- to make a grave for your ugly thoughts, and a garden for your kindly feelings?

Are you willing to do these things, even for a day? Then you can keep Christmas.

Are you willing
- to believe that love is the strongest thing in the world — stronger than hate, stronger than evil, stronger than death —
- and that the blessed life which began in Bethlehem...is the image and brightness of the eternal love?

Then you can keep Christmas.

Our children learned the words of a song from an old vinyl record album, *Merry Christmas from Sesame Street*, "Keep Christmas with you all through the year."

If we can keep Christmas for a day, why not always?

* * * * *

22.

SAINT NICHOLAS AND SANTA CLAUS

The closer we get to Christmas, the more I see of Santa Claus. I see his likeness depicted on sweaters, neckties, and billboards. A favorite Christmas ditty, "Santa Claus is Coming to Town," was written by John Frederick Coots and Haven Gillespie in November 1934. The song declares that Santa is everywhere.

> He sees you when you're sleeping.
> He knows when you're awake.
> He knows if you've been bad or good,
> So be good for goodness' sake.

Because Santa is so much a part of the holiday season, maybe we ought to know more about him.

The true story of Santa Claus begins with Nicholas, who was born late in the third century in the village of Patara located in what is now Turkey. His wealthy parents died in an epidemic while Nicholas was still young.

Nicholas had a heart of love for all people, especially the needy. Following the Gospel teaching to sell your possessions and give to the poor, he used his entire inheritance to assist the needy, the sick, and the suffering. Nicholas became a beloved priest. Children knew him for his kindness.

Beyond historical facts, legends about St. Nicholas abound. One recounts that Nicholas heard of the plight of an impoverished man. The man's three daughters were not eligible for marriage because they had no dowry. The culture dictated — no dowry, no husband. The poor man could have sold his daughters into slavery, but he refused. They would be his responsibility all of his life.

Moved with compassion, Nicholas rode on his white horse past the man's humble home. He tossed three bags of gold coins into an open window to provide a dowry for each of the three daughters. One of the bags of coins fell into a stocking that had been hung by the fireplace to dry. From this act of kindness developed the legend that St. Nicholas comes secretly to fill stockings with gifts.

We do know that Nicholas eventually became the Bishop of Myra. He dressed in the typical clothing of a bishop: a red cap and a long, flowing red robe. Following his death, he became St. Nicholas, canonized by the Roman Catholic Church. The feast day of St. Nicholas is December 6.

Throughout much of the world, December 6 is the day that children expect gifts from St. Nicholas. Typically, they place their shoes either outside the door or under the Christmas tree. The following morning, they find their shoes filled with candies, goodies, and small toys. It is a tradition that Clare and I adopted when our children were younger.

In France, St. Nicholas is called Père Noël. In England, he is simply known as Father Christmas.

The legend of St. Nicholas came to the United States through Dutch immigrants. He was known as Sinter Claus, a derivative of St. Nicholas in the Dutch language. In time, Sinter Claus became Santa Claus. Santa Claus, then, is a continuation of the legendary fourth-century priest who cared about children and the poor.

The priest who became St. Nicholas was actually a thin man. Over the years his image changed.

In 1931, the Coca-Cola Company in Atlanta, Georgia, used Santa Claus in some of their advertising at Christmastime. A graphic artist created an image that was based on the poem by Clement Moore entitled "The Night before Christmas." In the poem, the jolly old elf is described as smoking a pipe and having a tummy that "shook when he laughed like a bowl full of jelly." The commercialized Santa Claus became a plump, jovial symbol of overconsumption.

Several years before her death, my mother gave me a gift, a ceramic figure that depicts Santa Claus kneeling before the baby Jesus in the manger. Santa had doffed his cap and his hands are folded. He is bowing in prayer. I have found the image appropriate because it removes Santa Claus from the center of Christmas.

The best response we can make to Christ is to give to other people, just as the original St. Nicholas did. In the true spirit of Christmas and in the enduring legacy of St. Nicholas, we need to concentrate on those who are needy, those who are poor.

I believe in the fantasy of Santa Claus, but I also believe we need to recapture the original spirit of St. Nicholas.

For more than fifteen years, I have had the rare privilege of playing the part of Santa Claus at an annual gathering for our church family. The children present a Christmas musical program including a Nativity tableau. Then, Santa Claus, yours truly, enters the sanctuary with a hearty, "Ho! Ho! Ho!"

Santa sits in a chair and tells the original Christmas story. The children gather around, sitting on the floor, while Santa tells about the birth of Jesus from Luke Chapter 2. When the children hear the story told by Santa Claus, it has a special effect on them. When Santa bows his head to pray, the children take note.

Following the program, Santa lingers, allowing the children to crawl up on his knee and tell him what they want for Christmas. Then Santa Claus asks each child, "Do you know what I want for Christmas?" The children always look surprised. This is probably the first time they have ever heard Santa make a request of them.

"I want you and your family to remember that Christmas is the birthday of Jesus. For his birthday present, I want you do something kind for someone else."

Through the years, I have received occasional disapproval for playing the part of Santa. Some of my fellow clergy question whether this role is appropriate for a pastor. Others who want to do away with Santa Claus altogether believe my participation is nothing short of promoting a pagan tradition. I respectfully disagree on all counts.

The original St. Nicholas was a caring pastor whose heart's desire was to teach others about the love of Jesus. That is exactly my motive in playing the part of Santa.

If we can recapture the original intent of the loving man known as St. Nicholas, we will rediscover a part of the real joy of Christmas.

✻ ✻ ✻ ✻ ✻

23.

SANTA ALMOST GOT CAUGHT

Early on the morning of December 24, 1981, I awoke after far too little sleep. Standing next to my side of the bed was our eight-year-old son, Erik. I checked the alarm clock. It was not yet 6:00 A.M. The cold morning was still dark, and I was so very tired.

"Dad, it's Christmas Eve! Get up!"

I certainly can understand an eight-year-old being excited on Christmas Eve, but this was different. Erik was not just excited; Erik had a plan. He was determined to catch Santa Claus. He suspected that I was actually the beneficent Christmas Eve visitor. Erik announced his strategy. "I'm going with you everywhere you go today."

I followed a tradition learned from my dad and granddad when I was a boy. When my children asked, I always told them that I was Santa Claus. Telling the truth as a principle of parenting was ingrained in me. When the topic of Santa Claus came up at our house, I would declare, "You know, I really am Santa Claus." Then I would force a deep-voiced laugh, "Ho! Ho! Ho!"

Oddly enough, my children responded just the way I did when I was their age. "You're not Santa Claus!" they would say. Then they would give all of the reasons why I could not possibly be the jolly old elf.

"You don't have a white beard."

"You don't have a red suit."

"You don't have any reindeer."

"You can't make all of the toys for all of the boys and girls in the world."

"You don't have enough time to deliver all of the Christmas presents."

Never once did anyone say, "You're not plump enough to be Santa Claus."

When I said that I was Santa Claus, they never believed me, until they were ready.

On Christmas Eve 1981, Erik was almost ready.

Erik was our child who loved puzzles, riddles, and games. Figuring things out was recreation for him. He would take things apart to find out how they worked. His curiosity was matched only by his determination to work the puzzle, to understand the riddle, or to solve the mystery. On Christmas Eve 1981, he was determined to find out for himself who Santa Claus really was. He intended to catch jolly old Saint Nicholas red-handed.

Back in those days, we observed Christmas Eve with my larger family, including my seven brothers and sisters and all of their children. Beginning with brunch at my sister's home, we had a kind of progressive Christmas celebration that concluded sometime after supper.

In 1981, through all of the Christmas Eve activity, Erik was my constant shadow. "I'm going with you wherever you go today," he had vowed. And he did!

He followed me everywhere I went all day long, and I do mean everywhere. At one point in the day, I had to leave my family festivities to make pastoral hospital visits and run a couple of last-minute errands. Erik left his cousins at play to follow along with me. Not once did he let me out of his sight.

By the time we returned to our home at the end of a long day, I was exhausted. I built a fire in the fireplace and played Christmas music on the stereo. The children hung their Christmas stockings in their accustomed places, and then we had our family devotion and prayer together.

At bedtime Erik informed us, "I'm staying up with Dad." Clare was eight months pregnant with our only daughter, Betsy. Clare, along with our three other sons, retired upstairs to bed. Erik and I settled into the den for a long night of waiting and watching for Santa.

Erik wanted to play a game of Monopoly while we waited for Santa's visit. I hate Monopoly! We played an entire game until he finally captured all of my property and soundly defeated me.

Around 2:00 A.M. on Christmas morning, I said, "You know, Erik, Santa Claus doesn't like to be seen. He's a very private person. Maybe we ought to go to bed."

Erik was resolute, "You can go to bed if you want to, but I'm going to stay up."

I took a pillow from the sofa and stretched out on the floor. I put my head down and went sound asleep, a talent I have cultivated over the years.

At 6:00 A.M. on Christmas morning, Erik shook me. "Dad, wake up! It's time!"

I struggled awake, "Time for what, Erik?"

"It's time for you to be Santa Claus."

"What do you mean, Erik? I thought you were going to catch Santa Claus."

"Dad, I know it's you! Get up, and fix the stockings! Everybody else will be up soon!"

"Erik, I've never known Santa Claus to be this late. But he doesn't like to be caught. I wonder if he knew you were staying awake, and he decided to be sneaky."

"Dad, quit kidding around," he said, exasperated. "I know it's you. People at school told me it was you."

I got up off the floor and straightened myself out. We went to the kitchen, and each of us had a glass of orange juice. I could not help but admire the tenacity of my son. It is a trait to be desired.

"Erik, Santa Claus is a wise fellow. If he thinks somebody is trying to catch him, he can be pretty sneaky. Maybe we'd better look around."

We investigated as if we were two private detectives. Erik discovered a trail of Christmas candy leading out of our front door and followed it into the yard where it ended.

"Maybe we should follow the trail in the other direction," I suggested.

The trail of candy, like something out of *Hansel and Gretel*, took us to the door leading to our basement.

Erik clicked on the lights and crept cautiously down the stairs. Turning the corner at the bottom of the stairs, his eight-year-old eyes, bleary from an all-night vigil, beheld the spectacle of Christmas gifts, assembled and arranged neatly for each child. The stockings were stuffed to overflowing. There was even a basket of baby gifts for our fifth child, yet to be born, and a basket for Clare with her favorite foods and, of course, chocolate.

Erik turned to me in disbelief. "How did you do that?"

I gave him a hug as he found a letter from Santa Claus written in red ink.

Dear Erik,
You and your dad were busy having fun together in the den, so I decided to set up in the basement. I knew a smart boy like you could find the candy trail. I brought some gifts that I think you and your brothers will enjoy.

The 1500-piece puzzle is especially for you. You like to solve mysteries. The secret to the mystery of Santa Claus is love.

I have something I want for Christmas from you. I want you and your family to remember that the most important part of Christmas is the birth of Jesus. That is a great mystery, too. His birth is the way we understand God's love.

That is the greatest gift of Christmas, the best surprise of all. It is a puzzle that we can never solve. It is an act of love that we can only believe.

Erik, I love you very much.

Merry Christmas,

Santa

Santa Claus almost got caught that Christmas in 1981. It would have been alright, I suppose, if his secret had been discovered. But Santa doesn't like to be seen, even if it means quietly working in the basement all night long on December 23, even if it means barely making it into bed just a few minutes before an excited eight-year-old boy comes to awaken him before dawn on Christmas Eve.

It is one of the surprising mysteries of Christmas love.

* * * * *

24.
CHRISTMAS SURPRISES

When children make their list for Santa, they usually include several very specific requests — a scooter, a bicycle, a video game, a doll. They often conclude with a wish for some surprises. Christmas is all about surprises.

One year after the holidays, we received a very nice thank you note from our postman, which he had placed in our mailbox. He wrote to tell us how much he had appreciated our kind gift of chocolate brownies. He commented on how delicious they were and how much he and his family had enjoyed them. We were surprised! We had not left brownies in our mailbox for our letter carrier.

At that time, we lived in Winston-Salem, North Carolina. Our home was about fifteen miles from the church that I served. The trip from town to our house and back was not one our church members made lightly. If, for example, they came to our home to deliver a holiday package and found we were not there, they did not make a return trip. Leaving edible treats on our doorstep was not a good idea because of the abundant critter population around our wooded lot. On numerous occasions, parishioners and friends left Christmas presents in our rural mailbox.

To this day, we believe that a kind church member brought homemade brownies as a gift to our family. Finding that we were not at home, they left the delectable offering in our mailbox by the road. As the mailman delivered our mail the following day, he found the chocolate treats before we did. He received a gift that was a surprise in every way; a surprise to him and a surprise to us.

What is amazing about Christmas is the frequency with which these surprises occur.

My grandfather and I shared a special relationship. In 1962, the first Christmas after he died, I received an unexpected treasure. My grandmother gave me Pappy's pocketknife, a Boker Tree Brand with three blades. I had seen Pappy peel apples with that same knife, creating a long, red unbroken spiral cascading to the floor. I had seen him cut binders' twine and fishing line with that pocketknife. I had even seen him use the knife to whittle on his false teeth, trying to make his dentures fit his gums better. Receiving Pappy's knife was the highlight of my Christmas that year. It brought back a flood of memories. It is a cherished keepsake to this day.

Several years ago, a church in San Antonio, Texas, constructed a Nativity scene on the church lawn. Figures of Mary and Joseph, the shepherds and wise men, and a few animals had been cut from plywood and beautifully painted by members of the church. An orange crate lined with hay served as the manger.

Two days before Christmas, a custodian at the church was mowing the lawn. As he approached the crèche, weed trimmer in hand, he heard the cry of a baby. He moved closer. Cautiously peering into the orange crate, he saw a real, live baby!

The custodian ran excitedly to tell the church secretary. A mother of three, she rushed out to the Nativity scene. She knelt and tenderly lifted the infant, cradling him in her arms. The tiny Latino boy was wrapped in a tattered, old blanket.

Pinned to his blanket was a note, scrawled by a frightened mother. It concluded with one more surprise.

> Please take care of my child.
> His name is Jesus.

The pastor of the church reported that Christmas was unusual for his congregation that year.

The Department of Social Services assisted the church in locating the teenage mother. With the encouragement of the congregation, the young woman decided to keep her child. The amazing appearance of the baby boy rallied the church in a spirit of caring.

Christmas is full of surprises. That's the way it should be. That's the way it was on the first Christmas. Startled shepherds and travel-worn wise men, a weary mother Mary, and a bewildered Joseph were all astounded. So, too, was a waiting world.

Tradition holds that a Messiah was anticipated in ancient prophecy. But, God gave His greatest gift in an unexpected way, a vulnerable child born in a stable out back and cradled in a manger.

What a surprise!

*****

25.

THE MEANING OF GIFTS

On Christmas Eve, Jeff and his extended family gathered in the living room of his grandmother's home. The family had grown so large that they had decided to draw names instead of giving gifts to everyone. Aunt Ethel didn't want to draw names. She was a wealthy spinster who could afford to give everybody a gift. She seemed to delight in selecting gifts and wrapping them. A gift from Aunt Ethel was like a work of art. The boxes were beautifully decorated.

When Jeff received the elongated flat box decorated with a Styrofoam snowman, he thought he knew what Aunt Ethel had given him. In early December, she had phoned to ask Jeff what he preferred. He carefully opened the box, keeping the cleverly crafted snowman intact. He was horrified! His gift from Aunt Ethel was perhaps the ugliest necktie he had ever seen. It looked something like a Purina Dog Chow bag. The pattern of large red and white checks was made even more hideous by what seemed to be little yellow amoebae, one resting at the center of each red square.

Jeff's face must have revealed his shock and disappointment. Everyone in the room was astonished when he lifted the tie from the tissue paper in the flat box. Jeff looked into the empty box to be sure he hadn't missed something.

Aunt Ethel asked brusquely, "Don't tell me you don't like it." Then she added, "It's exactly what you said you wanted."

Jeff exclaimed, "Aunt Ethel, when you asked me if I preferred a large check or a small check, I didn't know you were talking about a necktie!"

The story of the magi tells of unusual people giving exotic gifts under strange circumstances. The gifts of gold, frankincense, and myrrh, as odd as they may seem, were actually quite appropriate. Gold is the gift for a person of royalty; frankincense is incense for a priest; myrrh is an embalming spice for one who is destined to die. In gift-giving it is not only the thought that counts; it is also the meaning behind the gift.

Well-chosen gifts need not be as extravagant as those of the wise men. One Christmas our children and I enjoyed building and giving bluebird boxes. The experience of making the nesting boxes, delivering the gifts, and knowing we were improving the environment brought triple satisfaction. Another year, I cut breadboards out of white pine, and Clare baked homemade bread to place on them. Our combined efforts made the gifts doubly personal.

Our family enjoys treasures that have been given to us in Christmases past. Cross-stitch pieces, knitted afghans, wooden serving trays, crocheted dish cloths, watercolor paintings, and hand-thrown pottery are pleasant reminders of friends and family who have taken the time to make a gift.

One smart fellow I know assembled paper ornaments and hung them inconspicuously on the tree. On Christmas morning, as presents were opened, the family wondered why there were no gifts from Dad. After all of the other gifts had been unwrapped, the father presented the paper ornaments to his family. Inside of each ornament was a personal note. To his son, he gave a three-day backpacking trip on the Appalachian Trail, just for the two of them. To his daughter, he gave a three-day skiing trip, just for the two of them. To his wife, he gave a two-week Caribbean cruise, just for the two of them.

The smart dad was a contemporary wise man. He not only gave presents to the people he loved, but he also gave the gift of presence, time to be spent with them.

The gift of presence is the heart of Christmas. The meaning of the divine covenant is that God dwells with His people. That gift is Immanuel, God with us.

That gift is better than any necktie or a check for any amount.

* * * * *

26.

THE BEST GIFTS

O. Henry, a master storyteller, was renowned for his surprise endings. One of his best-known stories is the Christmas tale "The Gift of the Magi." Allow me to remind you of the tale.

A newly married couple, James and Della Young were very much in love with each other. Because they were starting out with few resources, they had no extra money to purchase gifts for each other at Christmastime.

Jim wanted to give Della a set of silver combs for her long, beautiful, flowing hair. Della wished she could give Jim a gold chain for the fine gold watch he had inherited. As Christmas approached, try though they might, neither Jim nor Della was able to accumulate enough money to purchase a gift for the other. They each came up with a secret plan.

On Christmas Eve, Della had her lovely hair cropped short. She sold her tresses to be used to make wigs for other women. With the money she received, Della purchased a gold chain for Jim's treasured watch.

When Della arrived at her home that night, her husband was, to say the least, quite surprised to see the new hairstyle. Della reached in her purse and took out a small package, which she handed to Jim. When Jim opened his gift, he was astonished to see the gold watch chain. When Della encouraged him to attach the chain to his watch, Jim hesitated and then gave his present to Della.

Upon opening her gift, Della was flabbergasted. Jim's gift to her was a set of expensive filigreed silver combs. She wondered how her husband could afford such a fine gift. She could have used those silver combs when her hair was long. Then Della realized that Jim had sold his watch to purchase a gift for her. They laughed together at the irony of their Christmas gifts to each other.

The two gifts perfectly represent sacrificial love. Jim and Della received material gifts that were of little value for the moment. But the gift that endured was their love for each other.

I recall telling O. Henry's *Gift of the Magi* to our children. Betsy commented, "It's just like the *Sesame Street* story about Bert and Ernie."

As that story goes, Bert exchanged his paperclip collection for a soap dish to give to Ernie for his favorite rubber duckie to sit in. Ernie swapped rubber duckie for a cigar box to hold Bert's paperclip collection. Mr. Hooper, the storekeeper, handled both top secret deals.

On Christmas Day, just as Bert and Ernie realize the ramifications of their transactions, there was a knock at the door. Mr. Hooper had stopped by to deliver their Christmas presents. He gave Ernie his rubber duckie and Bert his paperclips.

The best gifts are selfless, and sometimes enduring gifts come from unexpected sources.

Gene Lassiter, the former pastor of Second Presbyterian Church in Spartanburg, had a custom of dropping by the church's Soup Kitchen from time to time. He often helped by serving the meals. Some of the people who ate meals at the Soup Kitchen came on a regular basis.

Gene told me a story about an encounter he had with one of those repeat visitors, a homeless man who often had multiple needs. Over the years, Second Presbyterian had ministered to this man in a variety of ways, but it was as if the church could never help him quite enough. I doubt if any church could have ever helped him sufficiently.

One Christmas Eve, the church held a worship service that concluded about 9:00 P.M. Gene had preached the sermon at that service, and he was the last to leave the church. Just as he was locking the door and removing the key, he looked up and saw this particular homeless man, walking across the lawn of the church directly toward him.

Gene just knew the man was going to ask for help once again, so he waited. The man walked up the steps to the church, reached out, and shook Gene's hand. Then he said, "Pastor Gene, I just came by to say thank you for the many things you have done for me and to tell you Merry Christmas."

With that, the man turned, walked back down the steps, and disappeared into the darkness of the night. Gene said he was astounded. The man had not made a single request on Christmas Eve. He had simply come by to express appreciation and to wish Gene a Merry Christmas.

The gift of gratitude is a special Christmas blessing.

One of my customs on Christmas Day is to visit those in our congregation who are ill and confined to the hospital. I have learned that they appreciate a brief visit on the holiday. The gift they value most is not a present. It is presence, simply being with someone who cares.

The heart of Christmas is the gift of presence, the gift of God's presence with us. The miracle of the incarnation is that the great God of creation came to be with us as a human being.

That's the best gift of all.

* * * * *

27.
CHRISTMAS AT CROFT

In 1946, when I was two years old, my parents were asked to leave the First Baptist Church of Spartanburg. That request had nothing to do with my being in the terrible two-year-old stage of childhood development.

They were sent to start a mission outside the Spartanburg city limits. First Baptist Church had purchased one of the several vacant chapels remaining at Camp Croft, an abandoned military facility where the United States Army had trained soldiers during World War II.

My dad, who ran a lumberyard as his regular work, had always been a devoted churchman. At Camp Croft Baptist Church, he did almost everything. He repaired the building, led the singing, and served as deacon chairman. He sometimes preached, and he prayed without ceasing.

Christmas at Croft was a happy time. One of the high points was the Sunday night in December when every young person in our church took part in the Christmas pageant. I was always asked to be a shepherd. Any boy who did not have one of the major parts — Joseph or a wise man — was automatically relegated to the role of shepherd. Any girl who did not have a major part — Mary or the Archangel — played the role of an angel in the heavenly host.

Being a shepherd was not hard. A shepherd did not need much equipment. Shepherds went barefooted. They wore their fathers' bathrobes and draped towels on their heads, which they secured with old neckties. Since my dad did not own a bathrobe, I had to wear my mother's red quilted robe.

The biggest concern for the shepherds was coming up with a suitable shepherd's crook design. At Croft we tried several models over the years. One Christmas, we made the staves out of heavy cardboard. They worked fine until it rained on them. Once they became soggy, they just flopped around.

Another year, the shepherd's crooks were made from broom handles and coat hangers bent into a hook. These worked just fine as dangerous weapons, but not so well for the Christmas pageant.

Finally, my dad made some top-of-the-line shepherd crooks out of quarter-inch plywood from the lumberyard. When all the shepherds gathered in the foyer of the church, we managed to have a sword fight or two. Those plywood staves sure made a lot of racket as they clacked together.

When I was ten years old, Gregory, who always played the part of Joseph, became ill with the flu. On Wednesday night before the Christmas pageant, the pastor's wife, who served as the director, asked me to take the role of Joseph.

This change in cast called for several major revisions. First of all, my mother's red quilted bathrobe, my attire in previous pageants, just would not do. The pastor's wife made me wear her husband's bathrobe, which was the most garish-looking robe imaginable. I felt as though I was wearing Joseph's coat of many colors. She rolled up the sleeves, bloused the robe above the belt so the back wouldn't drag across the floor, and cinched the belt tight. I was still allowed to go barefooted, but she insisted that I wear a fancy towel on my head. A white one was much too plain for Joseph. She wrapped a striped towel around my head and tied it with one of her husband's gaudy cast-off ties.

The biggest problem I faced was that I had to stand close to Jenny, the prettiest girl in the church. At that time in my life, I was scared of girls. Though Jenny was only a year or two older than I was, she looked like a grown woman. She had started filling out in all the right places. Standing close to Jenny would have been tough for a ten-year-old boy in any circumstance, but standing close to Jenny while wearing a bathrobe was almost more than I could stand.

All of the cast members, including me, practiced the pageant on the same night I found out that I was to be Joseph, the Wednesday night before the Christmas pageant. Several men in the church worked on the spotlights that were to be focused on the stage. Jenny and I walked down the aisle and took our positions. Jenny placed a Betsy Wetsy doll, which we were using as a substitute for Baby Jesus, in a manger made from scrap lumber.

Beverly, the Archangel, stood in the baptistry window. At Croft, as in most Baptist churches, the baptismal pool is located above and behind the pulpit and the choir loft. It was the perfect perch for an Archangel. From there Beverly shared good tidings of great joy. As the shepherds entered down the aisle, the heavenly host sang to them.

Finally, the wise men walked forward and presented their gifts: a cigar box wrapped in gold Christmas paper, an Old Spice Aftershave bottle, and a Witch Hazel bottle wrapped in tin foil.

We had rehearsed well. We were ready.

Then, on Saturday, Gregory called and demanded, "Kirk, I'm better now. I don't have the flu anymore. I'll be Joseph. I already know how to do it, and I can do it better than you." Gregory was sweet on Jenny.

I said, "No, I've practiced, and I think I can do it."

Gregory was a persuasive fellow. When I wouldn't budge, he talked one of the wise men into being a shepherd instead. If Gregory couldn't be Joseph, at least he could still be a part of the play as one of the magi.

The night of the pageant came. Shepherds, angels, wise men, Mary, and yours truly as Joseph gathered in the foyer of the sanctuary. Shepherds were clacking the plywood crooks together, and angels were fluffing their wings as they were led into a side room to await their entrance. Each group had a cue to enter the sanctuary. Jenny and I, as Mary and Joseph, would enter with Baby Jesus when we heard the pianist play the first strains of "O Little Town of Bethlehem."

Anxious to see inside the sanctuary before the pageant began, Jenny cracked the door open and peeked inside at the assembled worshippers.

She said with alarm, "Y'all, there are people in there! I've gotta' go to the bathroom!" She tossed me the baby doll and took off running.

She had been gone only a few minutes when the pianist began playing our cue, the carol "O Little Town of Bethlehem." I stood there with that Betsy Wetsy doll, not knowing exactly what to do. I did know that I could not walk in without Mary. Thinking that we had not heard our cue, the pianist started playing the second verse, this time much louder. I felt stranded, left holding an abandoned baby. Jenny returned soon afterward. I shoved the doll into her arms, and we hurried down the aisle together.

When Jenny laid Baby Jesus, the doll, in the manger, it issued forth a cry that sounded like a mad cat. I didn't remember the doll ever crying before during rehearsal. I got tickled and struggled trying desperately not to giggle out loud. After all, this was supposed to be a solemn occasion, a reenactment of the Christmas story.

Fighting to keep my composure while waiting for the shepherds to enter, I became aware that it was extremely warm in the crowded church. In those days, I used a product on my flattop haircut known as Butch Hair Wax. It was basically petroleum jelly with a faint aroma. I would comb that wax on my hair to make it stand up straight.

Between my nervousness about standing next Jenny, my attempt to control giggles, the glare of the spotlights, the warmth of a towel tied on my head, and the bulk of the pastor's bathrobe, my hair wax started to melt. I could feel it oozing down my forehead. I used the sleeve of the bathrobe to wipe the wax away from my eyes.

When the pianist began playing the carol "While Shepherds Watched Their Flocks by Night," the group of boys rattled down the aisle with their plywood staves. Beverly, the Archangel, appeared in the baptistry.

When the spotlight caught the silver braces on Beverly's teeth, it really did look as if the glory of the Lord was shining 'round about her. Most of us were sore afraid.

"Angels We Have Heard on High" marked the entrance of the heavenly host through the side door. During rehearsal, the angels had not practiced their entrance dressed in full costume. Their wings were made out of cardboard covered in gold foil. The border was edged in gold tinsel. No one had foreseen the problem the size of the wings would cause. With wings wider than the door, the first angel got stuck on the door jamb. A helpful mother backstage rushed over and turned each angel sideways before sending them through the door, one angel at a time.

"We Three Kings of Orient Are" signaled the magi to enter and present gifts to the Christ Child. They made their way down the aisle as the carol was played, one carrying the cigar box wrapped in gold paper and one carrying the Old Spice Aftershave bottle. Gregory followed.

He must have been about halfway down the aisle when he realized that he had forgotten to bring the Witch Hazel bottle. In his last-minute rush to get one of the main roles, he had left out one of the most important props – a gift. As I again wiped away Butch Hair Wax from my forehead with the sleeve of the pastor's bathrobe, I saw Gregory hike up his own bathrobe and fumble with something in his blue jeans pocket.

The wise men reached the front of the church and offered their gifts. The cigar box wrapped in gold paper was laid by the manger. The Old Spice Aftershave bottle was carefully put in place. Finally, Gregory placed at the feet of Baby Jesus his gift, his prized Duncan Spinner Yo-Yo.

I have often thought about that Christmas pageant at Croft. It certainly was different from the elaborate, professional plays presented in places like Oberammergau in Germany, the Crystal Cathedral in California, or the churches I have served since Croft.

In some ways, though, that Nativity pageant at Croft is more like the first Christmas than any of the others could ever be. The people in that first Christmas pageant in Bethlehem long ago were much like us. A young woman, probably a teenager, was about to have her first baby in a stable. A carpenter served as a midwife. Like the character Prissy in *Gone with the Wind*, he didn't "know nuthin' 'bout birthing no babies." Shepherds, the blue-collar workers of their day, were just minding their own business when they were overcome with fear, wondering what on earth, and what in heaven, had happened. And the magi, who hitched their caravan to a star, brought gifts as precious to them as a Duncan yo-yo is to a young boy.

The Christmas pageant at Croft always concluded with the congregation singing "Away in a Manger." A line in that carol says, "The Little Lord Jesus, no crying he makes." Just as surely as that Betsy Wetsy doll cried, I'll bet Baby Jesus cried, too.

I laugh, and I cry, every time I remember Christmas at Croft.

* * * * *

28.

SEARCHING FOR THE MANGER

A little girl looked forward to her ninth birthday on December 24. For several years her parents had combined her birthday party with a Christmas Eve gathering in their home. As the only child in the family, the little girl assumed that the festivities were all for her.

Few people bothered to wish her a happy birthday, fewer still brought gifts. Her beautifully decorated home was filled with partying adults. She thought that surely the guests had gathered in her honor.

Finally, the nine-year-old, feeling ignored and left out, shouted in frustration at the top of her lungs, "Hey, whose birthday is it anyway?"

The little girl's question is one that we might well ask ourselves as we approach Christmas. Whose birthday is it anyway? The little girl deserves her own birthday party, and so does Jesus.

To celebrate Advent is to come again to the stable and remember the one whose birth we celebrate. At the heart of Christmas is a child in a feeding trough, a manger that we must seek anew each year.

The search for the birthplace of Jesus began with the shepherds of Bethlehem. They were tending their flocks when the sky erupted in light and in song. Scripture says they were scared to death. Hearing that a Savior had been born, they went with haste to find the babe wrapped in swaddling clothes lying in a manger.

The magi from ancient Persia joined the search when they saw an unusually bright star, a sign in the night sky that a new person of royalty had been born. Following the star, they came to Bethlehem.

Beneath the altar in the Grotto of the Nativity in Bethlehem, a silver star marks the spot believed to be the birthplace of Jesus. Helena, the mother of the Emperor Constantine, identified the site and ordered the construction of a church there. The Church of the Nativity was completed in 333 A. D.

During the season of Advent, thousands of Christians journey to Bethlehem to visit the holy place where the manger cradled the Christ Child. The basilica is entered through a low door called the Door of Humility. The only way to visit the birthplace of Jesus is to stoop, crouch, or bend low.

In Christian tradition, Advent is a time of preparation. As expectant parents prepare for the birth of a child, so the Church has interpreted Advent as the days of getting ready for the birth of Christ. Advent calendars and wreaths help us count down the days until the holy birthday arrives.

A season filled with activity and a hectic pace may interfere with our spiritual preparation. We may be so busy decorating our homes, attending events, and shopping 'til we drop, that we have little time to focus on the spiritual significance of the season. A favorite carol reminds us, "Let every heart prepare Him room."

Recently, a family told me about their preparation for Christmas. "When we got the Nativity set down from the attic, the manger was missing. We don't know what happened to it. We couldn't find it anywhere." Finding the manger is important for all of us who celebrate the birth of Jesus.

A story originally told by Dr. Jess Moody from his experience while serving as Pastor of First Baptist Church of West Palm Beach, Florida, illustrates the importance of our quest.

In 1976, Jimmy Carter, the former governor of Georgia, was running for president. Mr. Carter had said that he was a born-again Christian. His statement created much discussion in the press and much concern from some people about his openness regarding his faith.

At a Democratic fund-raising event in Florida, Jimmy Carter was seated on the platform with Mrs. Rose Kennedy, the mother of former President John F. Kennedy.

Mrs. Kennedy leaned over and said, "Mr. Carter, I understand that you have been born again."

Mr. Carter answered, "That's right."

"So have I," Mrs. Kennedy declared.

Mr. Carter knew that she was a devout Roman Catholic. Evangelical Christians do not expect to hear Catholic Christians speak of being born again. Curious, he asked her to explain.

Mrs. Kennedy said that during the Christmas season following the death of her son Joseph, she was grieving deeply. She did not want Christmas to come. She did not want to celebrate.

A maid who worked in the Kennedy home couldn't help singing Christmas carols. The closer Christmas came, the more carols she sang. Finally, Mrs. Kennedy scolded, "Hush! I don't want to hear any more Christmas carols. I'm in no mood for Christmas."

The woman turned to her and said, "Mrs. Kennedy, what you need is a manger in your heart." Outraged, Rose Kennedy abruptly fired her maid.

Later that night, Mrs. Kennedy, feeling remorse, got down on her knees beside her bed and prayed that God would put a manger in her heart. God answered her prayer. The next morning, she called the woman and asked her to come back to work. Mrs. Kennedy encouraged the maid to sing all the Christmas carols she wanted.

If we believe that we are in a time of preparation, a time of waiting to celebrate again the birth of Christ, our prayer becomes

> O Holy Child of Bethlehem,
> Descend to us, we pray.
> Cast out our sin and enter in.
> Be born in us today.

The Church of the Nativity in Bethlehem is entered through the Door of Humility. So, too, is Advent. For Christians, Advent is the time to search for the manger, a quest that requires a posture of humility.

Wise men and wise women still kneel in humble adoration. When we do, we will find the manger.

Each of us will find it within our own heart.

* * * * *

29.

SENDING A BABY TO DO A MESSIAH'S JOB

In his Daily Study Bible commentary on the Gospel of Matthew, William Barkley explains the meaning of the gifts that the wise men brought to the Christ Child. Gold was the gift for a king. Frankincense was the gift for a high priest. Myrrh was an embalming spice for the Savior.

If you take just those three items and what they symbolize, you can see what a demanding job description the Messiah had. He was to be the King of Kings, the great High Priest, and the Redeemer of the whole world.

If that was the three-fold mission to be completed, why in the world would God appoint an infant for the task? Why send a baby to do a man's work? Why would God, in his infinite wisdom, expect a child to fill the role of Messiah? Yet, that is exactly what God did.

The reason God sent a baby is one of the great mysteries of Christmas. We find in the teachings of Jesus an answer to this question. Two passages from the Gospel of Mark give us a clue to the reason God would do such a thing.

Jesus asked his disciples, "What were you arguing about on the road?" Of course, they did not want to tell him because they were arguing about who among them was the greatest. Jesus did not press the point. Instead, he took a child in his arms and said, "Whoever welcomes one of these little children in my name welcomes me; and whoever welcomes me does not welcome me but the one who sent me" (Mark 9:36-37).

There is something special about receiving a child. If we can receive a child, we can receive the Christ Child. If we can receive Jesus, we can receive the great God of the universe.

Just one chapter later, we read that the disciples did not quite understand. In fact, parents were bringing little children to Jesus for his blessing, but the disciples rebuked them.

Jesus admonished the disciples and all who were within earshot, "Let the little children come to me, and do not hinder them, for the kingdom of God belongs to such as these. Truly I tell you, anyone who will not receive the kingdom of God like a little child will never enter it" (Mark 10:14-15).

What does Jesus mean when he says we must receive the kingdom like a child? I would suggest five options.

Certainly one possibility is that we must have a sense of wonder about life.

Now that we have grandchildren, Clare and I remember what it is like to see the world through the eyes of a child.

Children are fascinated that the moon seems to be moving all over the sky. One night it is here, and another night it is there. Some nights you cannot see it at all.

When I walk with one of our grandchildren, I see firsthand their sense of wonder about everything, from a frog on a rock to a honeybee on a flower, from a fish in a pond to a bird on a feeder. They take it all in. Walking with a child is like walking with God. You have to go slowly. You see things that you would never notice otherwise.

Wonder brightens their faces when they visit our home during the holidays. Do you know how a child's eyes gleam when exploring a Christmas tree? The feel of the needles, the fragrance of the branches, the twinkling lights, and the dazzling ornaments make the Christmas tree a marvel to behold. Do you know how fascinated a child can be with candles in an Advent wreath? The tapers magically ignite when a grandmother strikes a match. The flickering flame is hot. The light is extinguished by a single stroke of a brass snuffer. The mystery of Christmas is heightened by every simple tradition.

A second possible meaning to Jesus' statement that we must become as little children is that we must learn to trust.

Trust is learned when the people in our lives are trustworthy. Is there anything more precious than having a child fall asleep on our shoulder? That little one knows that we will provide protection and security. Children know that we can be counted on to take care of their needs. For a child, the world can be a frightening place. Dogs bark, big trucks roar past in the street, and stove tops burn. But there is a safe place in the world with mama and daddy, with grandmamma and granddaddy. That is how children learn to trust.

A third interpretation is that Jesus knew that little children must learn to obey. Children learn that they can depend on the adults in their world to tell the truth and to keep their promises. But trust and obedience go together. We sing the words "Trust and obey. There is no other way." Becoming as little children means that we learn the lesson of obedience.

In the fourth place, God might have sent a baby for another reason, too. When a newborn comes into our lives, everything changes.

I use a passage found in the Apostle Paul's letter to Corinth out of context: "Behold, I tell you a mystery. We shall not all sleep, but we shall all be changed" (I Corinthians 15:51 NKJV). We ought to display that verse as a humorous sign above the door of every church nursery and every child care center.

WE SHALL NOT ALL SLEEP, BUT WE SHALL ALL BE CHANGED.

A child changes our lives. God sent the child Jesus because he wants us to change. He wants us to be open to new possibilities.

Fifth and last, God wants us to be open to his love.

Every year as a part of our Christmas celebration we sing, "O, come to my heart, Lord Jesus. There is room in my heart for you." Every Christmas, we sing that we are going to receive Christ into our hearts: "Let every heart prepare him room."

Why in the world would God send a baby? Sending a child was the best way to get our attention. We come close to the manger and look into the face of this little child sent from God. We see the great resemblance to this baby's Father in heaven.

We see there not only what God is like but also what God wants us to be like. He wants us to grow in the image of Christ.

* * * * *

30.

MADONNA IN BLUE JEANS

Clare and I have friends with a remarkable story. Unable to have children biologically, the couple decided to adopt three children from a country in Asia. Before the adoption process was finalized, the young woman discovered that she needed a hysterectomy. As she went into surgery, she clutched a picture of the three children she intended to adopt.

On the Sunday before Christmas several years ago, the entire family came to Spartanburg for a visit. Clare and I met them for lunch at Cracker Barrel. As we waited on the front porch for our table, I watched this young mother rocking her three adopted children and reading to them. The tenderness in her face and the trust in her children's faces reminded me of the nurturing relationship at the heart of the Christmas story, the close bond between Mary and her child.

I have always been fascinated by the description of Mary as a woman with a pondering heart. As a teenage mother she had much to ponder, most of all the miracle she held in her arms and the responsibility of being his mother. In truth, the birth of every child is a miracle. Every child requires a lot of tending, even when that child is Jesus.

I miss my mother more at Christmastime than at any other time of year. She loved this season, decorating her home, hosting friends and family, and, as much as anything else, rocking her grandchildren.

One of the great comforts for me at Christmas is to see mothers and grandmothers holding little babies. So many Christmas cards depict Mary and Jesus, Madonna and child, in soft pastel tones. Many Christmas carols present the same picture. "What Child is this, who, laid to rest on Mary's lap, is sleeping?"

Little babies do sleep and are sometimes calm and peaceful, but they can also be quite demanding. Though he was the Son of God, Jesus was also fully human. In the familiar carol "Away in a Manger," I doubt that the line "no crying he makes" held true for very long.

The word *Madonna* is Latin for my lady. A part of Christmas for me is to take note of the real-life Madonnas in my world: our nieces cradling a great-nephew or great-niece; a young mother sitting on the front row of our sanctuary holding her newborn as she listens to the Christmas cantata; grandmothers taking delight in the third-generation offspring while giving new mothers a temporary break from the constant demands of parenting.

Among the most precious images of a Madonna in my life are the photos of our daughters-in-law holding their children. These visions of sweet young mothers cradling infants and young children resemble beautiful Christmas cards. Barefooted and wearing blue jeans, these women hold treasures — our grandchildren!

Beginning with Christmas 1970 and the birth of our son Mike, I have witnessed the love and care and constant attention of the finest mother I have ever known. When our children were very young, I would sometimes come home from a day of ministry to find a Carolina Madonna in blue jeans, faithfully carrying out the ministry God gave her. I have seen her care for our children, sacrificing her own needs. Clare frequently thinks about our two oldest grandchildren who live in New Hampshire and our grandchildren in Tennessee. She wants to be with them whenever possible, all the while enjoying those grandchildren who live in our hometown. The longer I am with Clare, the more I appreciate her and see in her the same maternal love so beautifully depicted in the face of Mary.

Heaven has a special place for women like this. I imagine it to be a place that looks something like the front porch of a Cracker Barrel restaurant with plenty of rocking chairs.

My mother and mother-in-law are there. Both of my grandmothers are there. Each woman is rocking and singing to a babe in her arms. And those women and those children experience Christmas, as one of our favorite carols puts it, "with great joy!"

For those who have lost a mother or a grandmother, Christmas can be difficult, especially if the loss is recent. It is my hope and prayer that you will catch a glimpse of a real-life Madonna and that you, too, will know the blessing of heavenly joy.

* * * * *

31.

G. I. JOE AND BABY JESUS

The benches in shopping malls were made for people like me. Even amidst frantic holiday consumers, if you give me a bench, a book, and a cup of coffee, I can become oblivious to any crowd, a survival skill learned as the oldest of eight children. In the days before Christmas with its distractions of sparkling tinsel and blinking lights, I am able to retreat into the pages of a paperback. Give me a place to sit and a good book, and I will enter a zone of solitude, deaf to the din around me.

Just before Christmas several years ago, Clare, our daughter, Betsy, and I made the unholy pilgrimage to a shopping mall, a cathedral of capitalism. Clare and Betsy both know that such a trip ranks among my least favorite activities. My attendance on this occasion was not optional. It was required. My responsibility was to be sure the cash registers jingled their accompaniment to the piped-in Christmas carols. I was excused to my bench and my book, resting in the assurance that I would be summoned at the proper time.

Before Clare and Betsy were ready for a late lunch, I realized I was in trouble. I had only one book, and this trip was becoming a two-book excursion. An hour and a half later, when I finished reading, I abandoned my spot and took up browsing.

My window shopping carried me past clothing stores and specialty shops and ended, as you might expect, in a bookstore.

There, the item that caught my eye was not a book at all. Near the checkout area at the front of the store, a Nativity scene was displayed prominently on a large table. The familiar depiction of the birth of Jesus was presented in large wooden figures that were handcrafted in Italy. For a person who loves wood and appreciates the art of carving as I do, the manger scene was fascinating. I might have held one of the figures in my hands to examine it more closely had it not been for the sign:

DO NOT TOUCH

On the way home from the mall, Betsy asked, "Dad, did you enjoy the day?"

I told her about the manger scene in the bookstore.

"Too bad about that sign," she replied. "Manger scenes were meant to be touched."

In 1223, Saint Francis of Assisi placed a crèche, a miniature Nativity scene, in a church in Grecchio, Italy. That was the beginning of a cherished Christmas tradition for many Christians.

Our family displays several Nativity scenes at various places in our home during the season of Advent. They help us keep our focus on the center of our Christmas observance. My mother made and hand painted a ceramic scene as a Christmas gift when we were first married. We display it on a mirrored sideboard in the dining room.

Over the years, we have accumulated an assortment of manger scenes that are intended for children to enjoy. One is made from two-by-fours, cut and sanded to resemble the Holy Family. In another, the figures are small stuffed dolls, sewn together from printed fabric and filled with batting. When our children were younger, they molded a set from clay. All are placed on low tables to invite touching.

A sturdy, store-bought Nativity occupied our coffee table for many years. When our children were small, I often came home after a day of pastoral work to find Fisher-Price toy figures — firefighters, police officers, doctors, and construction workers — placed next to shepherds as if they, too, had heard the angels' message and paused from their work to worship.

I have seen Luke Skywalker, Han Solo, Princess Leia, and other *Star Wars* action figures standing next to the magi. It was as if they, too, had followed the new star from "a galaxy far, far away" through a time warp all the way to Bethlehem.

Several years ago, in our worship service on the first Sunday of Advent, a couple in our church lit the first candle in the Advent wreath, the candle of hope. Their son was a West Point graduate commissioned as a lieutenant in the United States Army. He had already served two tours of duty in Iraq and was in Baghdad at the time. To see them lighting the candle of hope at the front of the sanctuary was a moving experience for the entire congregation.

During the Christmas season, the frequency of war in our world has renewed a vision indelibly etched in my memory. I recall descending the stairs in our home one December morning years ago to find G. I. Joe action figures arranged in the manger scene on the coffee table. The miniature Joe and several of his well-armed buddies circled the perimeter of the crèche. The small soldiers were facing outward, as if standing guard.

With delighted curiosity I asked our children, "Tell me the story about this."

"King Herod wants to kill Baby Jesus," came the explanation. "G. I. Joe and his guys are protecting him."

Through the day, the model military force protected the Holy Family. That night, after everyone else had gone to bed, I sat before the Nativity and pondered. Maybe Christians do need to protect Baby Jesus, not from Herod and his Roman soldiers, but from an internal, invisible enemy, from anything that would eliminate the Christ from our lives.

It occurred to me that our role in Christmas is not just to protect Baby Jesus in his vulnerability. Christians have another, more important imperative, to worship the Child who is the Son of God.

Sitting alone in the dark, in an act of private unilateral disarmament, I carefully removed the weapons from G. I. Joe and his comrades. I reshaped their pliable bodies. Then giving them an about-face, I switched them from an outward attack position and turned them to face the manger. The plastic soldiers knelt beside shepherds and wise men in humble adoration of the Prince of Peace.

* * * * *

THE NEW YEAR

32.

THE TWELVE DAYS AFTER CHRISTMAS

Is there anything as over as Christmas? Colorful wrapping paper and bright ribbons are reduced to trash as quickly as gifts are torn open. Fresh green trees that have graced our homes for weeks begin to drop needles until they are discarded along city streets, waiting like fallen soldiers to be collected by the body wagon. Even artificial trees are stored in plastic containers the size of coffins. Decorations are packed away in the basement, the attic, or the garage until next year.

Christmas is over!

In the week following Christmas, we may become preoccupied with returning and exchanging gifts, cleaning house, and paying bills. No wonder the days after Christmas mark a mood swing. The season to be jolly often dissolves into a time of exhaustion and despair.

The post Christmas season can also be a time of blessed relief. For those who enjoy gardening, the mail carrier brings not only bills and tax forms, but also seed and plant catalogues.

The days between Christmas and New Year's Day give us time for reflection on the year past and the year ahead. Opening a new calendar can be an opportunity to plan and organize by marking birthdays, anniversaries, vacations, and other special occasions. Stretching nonstop into the foreseeable future are bowl games for avid football fans.

December 26 is Boxing Day. It primarily observed throughout the United Kingdom and former Commonwealth countries. In Ireland it is called St. Stephen Day. In the English tradition the day is a time to offer presents to the people upon whose service we depend all year, those who deliver our newspaper and our mail, bag and carry groceries for us, clean our offices, and service our automobiles, just to name a few.

The twelve days of Christmas include Boxing Day and end on Epiphany, January 6. These twelve days after Christmas provide an opportunity to extend the holidays.

The song "The Twelve Days of Christmas" is based on this season of gift-giving. If we assume a partridge in a pear tree is given only on the first day and each of the other gifts are given only once, the monetary value in dollars at this writing would be about $20,000.

However, the song implies that the gifts given each day are repeated on each of the remaining eleven days. By January 6th, the recipient would have a total of twelve partridges and twelve pear trees. By the twelfth day, the beloved would have received 376 gifts, including 184 birds. Then the cost at this writing would be about $75,000.

Some Christians believe that the song was actually a catechism in disguise, used by English Catholic parents to teach their children during the time of Puritan rule in Britain.

- The partridge in a pear tree represents the one true God.
- The two turtledoves are the Old and New Testament.
- The three French hens symbolize the Trinity.
- The four calling birds are the four Gospels of Matthew, Mark, Luke, and John.
- Five golden rings are the first five books of the Bible, known as the Torah.
- Six geese a-laying refer to the six days of creation.
- Seven swans a-swimming are the seven sacraments.
- Eight maids a-milking are the eight beatitudes.
- Nine ladies dancing are the fruits of the Holy Spirit.
- Ten lords a-leaping represent the Ten Commandments.
- Eleven pipers piping are the eleven faithful apostles.
- Twelve drummers drumming are the twelve doctrines in the Apostle's Creed.

All trivia aside, the twelve days after Christmas can have a deeper meaning.

A young father, a member of the congregation I served in North Carolina, was stricken by leukemia and hospitalized for several weeks just before Christmas. Because Stan's immune system was compromised, his physician would not permit his two small children to visit their father.

When I visited with Stan on Christmas Day, his disease was in remission. He was looking forward to being discharged from the hospital. "We're going to have Christmas when I get home," he said in anticipation.

Stan left the hospital two days later. He and his wife gave each child one present every day for the next week or so. Spreading out the gifts conserved Stan's energy and enabled the family to extend Christmas into the New Year. Sadly, Stan died later that same year.

One year, in early December, Stan's daughter, an adult by then with children of her own, spoke with me. "I remember that Christmas, the last one with my daddy, as the best one ever. Instead of the whole thing suddenly being over as it usually is, Christmas seemed to last and last."

The twelve days after Christmas need not be a season of despair. In the afterglow of Christmas, joy and peace can accompany us into the New Year.

* * * * *

33.

OUT WITH THE OLD! IN WITH THE NEW!

As I mentioned in Chapter 5, "The Inviting Table," our family, like so many others in the South, gathers on New Year's Day for a meal as traditional as watching football games. Pork chops, black-eyed peas, collards or turnip greens, and cornbread is the fare. Southern lore holds that anyone eating such a meal on January 1 will enjoy prosperity in the year ahead. Dad's custom was to give each person a two-dollar bill. It was his way to give us all a jump-start on the anticipated good fortune. He always said, "If you don't spend this, you'll never be broke."

I have continued the tradition of giving out two-dollar bills to our children and grandchildren.

The Romans depicted Janus, the god of doors and gates, as a deity with two faces: one looking backward, the other looking forward. The two-faced god, holding keys, presided over new beginnings. The month of January in the Julian calendar was named for Janus. The first day of the first month was his sacred day. Janus characterizes all of us at this time of year. We look back at the year that is ending. We look forward to the year ahead.

As a teenager, I remember that the last week of the year was the time to take inventory at our family's lumberyard. Out of school for the holidays, I was available to help count fir and pine framing stacked on the yard, plywood in a warehouse, and moulding and trim in the dark bins of a lumber shed.

The concept of a year-end inventory has stuck with me through the years. What have been some of the blessings of the past year? My personal list is always lengthy and includes family and friends. Every year has times of difficulty, to be sure, but even those present opportunities and reasons to be grateful.

A January ice storm, a common occurrence in my neck of the woods, is a good example of the bittersweet mixture of difficulty and blessing as the new year begins. Fractured trees and downed electrical lines leave many homes and businesses without power. In the midst of chaos, we see, yet again, the best spirit of our community. Law enforcement and fire department personnel, essential utility employees, and emergency medical workers labor long hours to put things back to normal as quickly as possible. A part of taking inventory is remembering to be thankful for the blessings that accompany difficulty.

We describe a new beginning as turning over a new leaf or starting with a clean slate. A new calendar presents us with 365 new leaves and 365 clean slates. It gives us the opportunity to plan ahead for events that have top priority. Marking special birthdays and anniversaries on a new calendar serves as a reminder to save those days. Blocking out time in advance for vacations and other family occasions guards against the inevitable avalanche of routine daily activities that can crowd out even the most important events.

Several years ago, I was headed out the door for a New Year's Eve Watch Night communion service at church. We had entertained a houseful of teenagers earlier in the evening. We had filled two large plastic trash bags with empty pizza boxes and discarded paper products. Clare asked if I would take the accumulated debris out of the house. I stuffed the black bags into the trunk of my car and dashed to church in time for the service, delaying the dumping of the refuse.

Following the service, which ended past midnight, I drove home, completely forgetting about the unsavory cargo in the trunk of my vehicle. New Year's Day and the day after came and went.

On January 3, I opened my car door again for the first time since very early New Year's morning. The three-day-old garbage made my vehicle smell like a sanitation truck. I had made a mistake that many of us make in our own personal lives. I had literally carried last year's garbage into the new year!

A new beginning calls for focusing on the blessings rather than on the difficulties of a year now past. We have the opportunity to make important decisions about how we will spend the gift of time in the year ahead. We also have the opportunity to dispose of last year's emotional and spiritual garbage, leaving behind past hurts and grudges.

Janus, the two-faced god of Roman mythology, presided over beginnings and endings. But, for Christians it is God who is the sovereign ruler of all time and eternity to whom we commit the new year.

A favorite hymn includes the words, "Take my moments and my days, let them flow in ceaseless praise." It is a prayer for a new beginning.

Out with the old! In with the new!

* * * * *

34.

ON MAKING AND KEEPING RESOLUTIONS

The beginning of the new year brings with it a flurry of resolutions, ranging from the impossible to the foolish. Many pledges and promises will be short-lived and will meet with mixed results.

A man in Georgia resolved to win the lottery. He spent so much money on tickets that his exasperated wife left him.

A woman in New York resolved to adopt a new pet every month. Her landlord soon evicted her from her apartment.

Most of us have had the unhappy experience of making resolutions we could not keep. Failure to honor our goals has often left us feeling guilty.

Here are some tongue-in-cheek suggestions that should be relatively easy for us to keep.

1. Gain weight, at least 20 pounds.
2. Stop exercising.
3. Read less. It makes you think too much.
4. Watch more TV.
5. Procrastinate more. Start next week.

The new year is both a time for looking back and for anticipating the year ahead. It's a time to reflect on the changes that might improve our lives and to resolve to make those changes. According to *Time.com* in January 2011, the top ten New Year's resolutions made by contemporary Americans are also the ones we have the most difficulty keeping. This list may help you consider your goals for the coming year.

1. Lose weight and get fit.
2. Quit smoking.
3. Learn something new.
4. Eat a healthier diet.
5. Manage money.
6. Spend more time with family and friends.
7. Reduce stress.
8. Make better use of time.

9.   Simplify by getting organized.
10. Quit drinking.

Three psychiatrists at the University of Maryland Medical Center, who are also professors of psychiatry, advise that the key to achieving even the loftiest goals is to get started immediately. Allow action to precede motivation. Don't wait until the mood seems right. Begin now! University experts offer these additional tips for keeping New Year's resolutions:

- Be positive. Avoid perfectionist thinking. While we certainly want to better ourselves, it is healthier to think in positive terms than it is to focus on how much we fall short of our aspirations.
- View setbacks as lessons for growth. Mistakes can be, and usually are, opportunities for learning. If you fall short of your goals, ask yourself what hindered you from achieving them. Then try to make corrections. People who like to sail understand this navigational concept. You almost never go directly from point A to point B. You set a course, take readings of your position, and then make adjustments as you go along.
- Make resolutions that are flexible and realistic. Avoid words like never and always in your resolutions. Think in terms of gradual, steady improvement.
- Share your goals with trusted friends. They can gently nudge you in the right direction when you veer off course. Accountability contributes to success.
- Give your resolutions personal meaning. Your goal should be something you really desire to change or achieve, not just something that others say will be good for you. You can be successful with strong, internal motivation.
- Set realistic goals that are attainable. Take small steps that are likely to be met with success. Rather than trying to lose ten pounds in a week, join a weight loss program instead. Try to lose one pound a week.
- Acknowledge the spiritual dimension of your goals. A good resolution will honor your physical, emotional, mental, and spiritual dimensions.

In my personal experience with New Year's resolutions, I am more likely to be successful if the goal is not simply self-improvement. A higher goal is to make life better for others, as well as for ourselves. A few examples may prompt a similar sense of resolve for you. This is a list I have honed over the years.

1. Express more appreciation for others. Make opportunities to offer a simple thank you. A word of encouragement affirms others and reduces stress for them and for us.
2. Perform random acts of kindness. These gifts of grace ease the way for others.
3. Plant a tree or a few flowers to brighten a corner of the world.
4. Recycle. Doing so helps the environment and raises our awareness.
5. Give a handshake, a hug, or a pat on the back. Kneel when you speak with a child. Call a person by name and look them in the eye. Personal contact enhances life.
6. Vote. Your voice makes a difference for us all.
7. Obey the law, especially when driving. Everybody benefits.
8. Pray beyond your own circle of concern. Impart hope to others.

The best resolutions are not so much the ones that make us better individuals, but those that make the world a better place for us all.

For several years I have enjoyed using the daily devotion book *Forward Day by Day.* It is a quarterly publication of Forward Movement (412 Sycamore St., Cincinnati, OH 45202), an agency of the Episcopal Church. Every issue includes a section entitled "Morning Resolve" that has become a part of my prayer life each day.

A Morning Resolve for Every Day

I will try this day to live a simple, sincere and serene life, repelling promptly every thought of discontent, anxiety, discouragement, impurity, and self-seeking; cultivating cheerfulness, magnanimity, charity, and the habit of holy silence; exercising economy in expenditure, generosity in giving, carefulness in conversation, diligence in appointed service, fidelity to every trust, and a childlike faith in God.

In particular I will try to be faithful in those habits of prayer, work, study, physical exercise, eating, and sleep which I believe the Holy Spirit has shown me to be right.

And as I cannot in my own strength do this, nor even with a hope of success attempt it, I look to thee, O Lord God my Father, in Jesus my Savior, and ask for the gift of the Holy Spirit. Amen.

* * * * *

35.

A NEW YEAR'S TREASURE HUNT

The Sacramento Bee carried an interesting article one New Year's Day. On January 1, 2008, Keith Severin and his seven-year-old son, Adrien, agreed to spend at least fifteen minutes every day together searching for treasure during the coming year. The father and son kept their promise. Each day, no matter the weather or the hectic schedule, they spent time together looking to see what they could find. At the end of the year, they proudly displayed their collection of coins, golf balls, tennis balls, recyclable bottles and cans, and various other items. In all, their treasure hunt yielded more than $1,000 worth of finds. The best value was the time of companionship and fun Keith and Adrien had together.

A treasure hunt is an apt metaphor for life. Some people buy a lottery ticket daily. Others make a habit of shopping every sale that comes along. Some folks spend most Saturdays driving from one yard sale to the next. Still others visit all the flea markets they can find. Many fill out entry forms for *Reader's Digest* or Publishers Clearing House Sweepstakes. I know one dad who pays his children to fill out sweepstakes entries.

Very few people win the lottery. Only a small minority will ever glean extraordinary value from items appraised on *Antiques Roadshow*, a Public Broadcast Service (PBS) production. Most who enter a sweepstakes will never hit the jackpot. But, all of us can discover treasures in the new year.

Russell H. Conwell gave a speech many times entitled "Acres of Diamonds." Conwell's speech included a parable about a man who searched the entire world looking for a precious jewel. Finally, he returned to his home, weary and discouraged. It was there that he discovered, in his own backyard, acres of diamonds gleaming in the sun.

Let me suggest three places to search for treasure during the coming year.

One place we will find treasure is in our own family and our church family. Others are the real treasures in our lives. They enrich us with love and acceptance.

We can discover treasure in the pages of the Bible. "If you seek her [wisdom] as silver, and search for her as hidden treasures, then you will understand the fear of the Lord" (Proverbs 2:4-5 NKJV). The regular reading of God's word yields nuggets of truth and wisdom in every chapter.

Finally we can seek treasure in the life of prayer. A close relationship with God is priceless. Jesus said, "Where your treasure is, there will your heart be also" (Matthew 6:21). Jesus went on to add, "Seek first the kingdom of God and his righteousness, and all of these things will be yours as well" (Matthew 6:33). We discover real treasure when we search for God through prayer.

Remember that God is also searching for us. It may have been at the turning of the year that Moses reminded the people of Israel, "The eyes of the Lord are always on you, from the beginning of the year to the very end of the year" (Deuteronomy 11:12, Author's Paraphrase).

Every new year promises to be a rewarding year, a year of treasure, if we look in the right places. I pray God's blessings for you and your loved ones in the year ahead.

I conclude with three prayers written by three different anonymous authors. You may find these meaningful as you enter the year ahead.

1.

May God make your year a happy one!
Not by shielding you from all sorrows and pain,
But by strengthening you to bear it, as it comes;
Not by making your path easy,
But by making you sturdy to travel any path;
Not by taking hardships from you,
But by taking fear from your heart;
Not by granting you unbroken sunshine,
But by keeping your face bright, even in the shadows;
Not by making your life always pleasant,
But by showing you when people and their causes need you most,
and by making you anxious to be there to help.
God's love, peace, hope, and joy to you for the year ahead. Amen.

2.

Heavenly Father, for this coming year just one request I bring.
I do not pray for happiness or any earthly thing.
I do not ask to understand the way you lead me;
But this I ask — teach me to do the thing that pleases thee.
I want to know your guiding voice,
To walk with you each day.
Heavenly Father,
Make me swift to hear and ready to obey;
And thus the year I now begin
A happy year will be,
If I am seeking just to do
The thing that pleases thee. Amen.

3.
Dear Lord, please give me…
A few friends who understand me and remain my friends;
A work to do which has real value,
without which the world would be the poorer;
A mind unafraid to travel, even though the trail be not blazed;
An understanding heart;
A sense of humor;
Time for quiet, silent meditation;
An awareness of the presence of God;
The patience to wait for the coming of these things,
With the wisdom to recognize them when they come. Amen.

* * * * *

36.

TREASURES OF SNOW

The month of January ushers into our lives, not only the promise of a new year, but also the prospect of winter weather. Meteorologists know that forecasting weather for the Upstate is always a challenge. Accuracy in their work becomes high risk in winter. With advanced technology at their fingertips and instruments of their trade close at hand, most weather professionals would agree with Jack Roper, a veteran weather forecaster in our community. He says that the tool that would be most helpful to them is the one usually absent in their weather room. They probably would be more accurate in their predictions if they only had a window. They could at least look outside to see for themselves what was actually happening.

Country folks have their time-honored ways of determining the long-range forecast. The length of hair on a horse's back or the colors of the fuzz on a wooly worm are indicators of the winter ahead. The relative scarcity or abundance of acorns, pecans, hickory nuts, and beechnuts are portents of the severity of winter.

In our part of the world, ice is the most dreaded winter weather event. A forecast of sleet and freezing rain is reason for concern. While ice covered trees have a crystalline beauty, the popping of breaking limbs and the cracking of splitting trunks are sounds of nature's agony. Frozen roads, slippery sidewalks and ice-laden power lines contribute to the human agony of broken limbs and splitting headaches.

During an especially severe ice storm several years ago, electric power at our house was out for several days. A friend called to add his unique brand of humor to the cold and dark. "This is the devil," he announced over the phone. "It's frozen over down here, too."

On the other hand, many people in the South, especially schoolchildren and schoolteachers, greet the prospect of snow with wild excitement. When the seven-day forecast held the promise of snow last winter, I asked a school principal, "Is it supposed to snow?" "It's always supposed to snow!" came the ready reply. A snow that sticks, that is, a snowfall with accumulation, creates a delightful playground. Snow angels, snowmen, snowballs, snow ice cream, and sledding are all fun, though fleeting, possibilities.

Some of our town's northern transplants are baffled by our enthusiastic reaction to snow. Enough is enough for them. Snow is an inconvenient nuisance.

They are annoyed and disdainful that a few inches of snow can bring life to a screeching halt for so many of us.

The truth is that people of the South do behave in strange ways when snow is impending. Grocery store shelves are quickly depleted of milk and bread. It was always difficult for me to understand why. Did hundreds of people sit in their homes eating bread and drinking milk because we had snow? I posed the question while standing in the express line at a grocery store several years ago. Snow was in the forecast. The woman ahead of me made sense out of what seemed like nonsense. "If my power goes out, I can give my three children peanut butter and jelly sandwiches and a glass of milk. The peanut butter and milk give them complete protein." I was glad to have a reasonable answer as I stepped forward to purchase my own bread and milk.

Dr. Alastair Walker, longtime senior pastor of a church I previously served, had a favorite sermon for just such an occasion. His text was from Job, in which the Lord asks Job, "Hast thou entered into the treasures of the snow?" (Job 38:22 KJV).

Dr. Walker had three points to his sermon. (1) No two snowflakes are alike. As the Creator fashioned each snowflake uniquely, so, too, has he created us. (2) Snowflakes are small and delicate, inconsequential as individuals. When many snowflakes accumulate, the world is altered by their combined power. So, too, can individual Christians, ineffective when acting alone, do marvelous things for God when working together. (3) Snow is instant urban renewal. A blanket of snow makes a dark, drab landscape bright and beautiful. Lives that are darkened by sin can become whiter than snow through God's forgiveness. Dr. Walker's three points identify the treasures of the snow.

My experience is that for children and adults alike, winter weather provides a day of grace, the unexpected blessing of free time. It can be an opportunity to enjoy our families. My mother always fixed a big pot of vegetable soup when schools closed because of snow. Though the roads were too dangerous to go to classes, her grandchildren found a way to get "over the river and through the woods to grandmother's house."

Even if the power goes out, this can be a time to sit by a hearth and read a book.

This day of grace is a time to think of others. As winter weather approaches, I try to remind our members to check on family and friends, especially those who live alone. Some time back, a man in our church made a special gift to our benevolent fund. "When I served in World War II, I was so cold I didn't think I would ever be warm again," he explained. His gift was used that very week to provide heating oil for a family of five that included three small children.

Two years ago, I was visiting the hospital during an ice storm when I came upon a homeless man sleeping in the stairwell. Winter weather is not a delight for everybody. It can be a reminder to those of us who have food and warmth to share. Organizations such as homeless shelters and soup kitchens provide service to our most needy citizens.

Winter weather can be a call to prayer for people of faith. If we receive a day of grace, some of that time can be spent in prayer. Remember those who are working while others have the day off. Medical personnel, paramedics, firefighters, law enforcement officers, utility employees, road crews, and tow truck drivers are but a few examples of those who labor long hours in the cold and damp. To remember them in prayer with petitions for their safety and gratitude for their service is our privilege.

I was working in Winston-Salem when a youth pastor there wanted to take students to a retreat after Christmas. The minister decided to take the group to Boone, North Carolina, for a snow skiing trip at a mountain resort.

When he and the thirty students arrived, nobody was on the slopes skiing. The manager of the lodge announced, "There's not going to be any skiing today. We have plenty of snow, but the ski lifts are not working."

The youth director had driven the group in a church van about two and a half hours. The deposit had been prepaid, and the group did not want to turn around and go home. Some of the youth asked, "Can we just play in the snow?" The manager saw nothing wrong with that idea, so after returning the deposit, he allowed the students to play in the snow while the minister and chaperones drank coffee by the fire.

After a while, the manager told the adults, "I want y'all to look at this." The youth minister and chaperones walked outside the ski lodge and saw the entire side of the mountain covered with snow angels. Those students had run up and down the side of the mountain, making snow angels. They took a situation that was disappointing and converted it into an experience of absolute joy.

These treasures of the snow come to all of us as gifts. When Erik died in November of 2000, our grief was profound. Spartanburg received a surprise snowfall with a slight accumulation on the day of Erik's funeral. Some expressed sadness that we had to have his burial in the snow. We felt differently. When we first saw the flakes falling gently from heaven, Clare said, "I think maybe Erik asked God for a favor. 'Lord, you know this will be a difficult day for my family. Could you please surprise them?'"

Like every good and perfect gift, snow comes from above. A Southern snowfall has become for us a blessing, a symbol of God's grace.

* * * * *

37.
JASON'S STORY

On New Year's Day 2005, I conducted an afternoon wedding. Returning to my office following the ceremony, I found a young man waiting for me. I did not recognize him.

"Are you Pastor Neely?" he asked. I introduced myself. He gave me his real name, but I will call him Jason. He asked, "Do you have time to talk with me?" I invited him into my office.

Jason explained that he was just walking past the church when he saw all the cars. He found his way into the church through an open door, discovered the wedding, and decided to wait for me. "It's New Year's Day," he commented, "and I want to talk with a pastor. I'm ready to turn over a new leaf."

I settled back to hear Jason's story. I thought he must be in his mid-thirties, but his gaunt face and slender body showed wear and tear far beyond his years. Jason, who grew up in South Carolina, was a high school athlete before he became a high school dropout. "My mom died when I was in the eighth grade," he explained. "I could never do anything right for my dad. My best was never good enough for him."

Jason enlisted in the U. S. Marine Corps to try to please his father. He served in Desert Storm. "I wanted to re-up, but they wouldn't let me. I think they knew I was gay." After discovering that his son was gay, Jason's father disowned him.

Jason had been living in Atlanta for almost ten years. "I did all the wrong things," he confessed. He returned to his hometown soon after Christmas because he had received word that his father had lung cancer. "He's been a lifelong smoker," Jason said. "I tried to get him to quit, but he never did." I noticed a pack of Marlboros in Jason's shirt pocket.

The trip home was a disappointment to Jason. Though dying, Jason's father still had little to do with his son.

"My dad is real sick, and so am I." Jason continued, "I found out I was HIV-positive a couple of years ago. Now I have AIDS."

In forty-five years of pastoral ministry, I have learned that trying to fix blame for human suffering is neither helpful nor redemptive. But, Jason had, in his own mind, accepted the unfair stereotype about AIDS being divine retribution upon gay men. He believed that God was punishing him for his life choices.

"The way I figure," Jason explained, "I deserve AIDS the same as my dad deserves lung cancer. Doesn't the Bible say we reap what we sow? My dad and I are both going to die. I don't think either one of us has very long. My dad says he's going to heaven. I want to be sure I'm there, too, even though he thinks I'm going to hell. I believe that heaven is my best chance to make things right between us, but first, I want to be sure I make things right with God."

I spoke with Jason about his faith. He had grown up in a Baptist church, where he was a member of the youth group. As a teenager, he had been baptized.

Jason came to me on New Year's Day to confess and receive the forgiveness of God. We prayed together before he left to hitchhike to Atlanta. Jason wept and thanked me. I shed a few tears of my own and bid him goodbye.

Jesus offered forgiveness instead of condemnation to a woman caught in adultery. He embraced the leper before he healed him. Some have said that AIDS is the present-day equivalent of leprosy in Jesus' day. While people with AIDS are not immediately identifiable and AIDS cannot be contracted by casual contact, the stigma that AIDS patients carry is similar to that of first century lepers. Jason wanted what every person of every age wants. He simply wanted to be loved.

Jason did not stop at the church and wait for me on New Year's Day to ask for money or medicine. He did not ask for transportation.

He wanted a new beginning. Though he gave few details, he wanted to confess, and he asked for the gift of forgiveness. I had the privilege of being the pastor Jason chose at random to hear his story and to offer the assurance of God's grace.

Jason's visit was a gift to me. It gave me the opportunity to form a new resolve.

My New Year's Day prayer every year is that God will grant to me what the Apostle Paul called the mind of Christ: to view others with the eyes of Jesus, to hear others with the ears of Jesus, to love others with the heart of Jesus, and to respond to others with the spirit of Jesus.

Will Jason and his dad ever be reconciled?

Only heaven knows for sure.

* * * * *

EPIPHANY

38.

THE MEANING OF EPIPHANY

Epiphany brings to a close the Advent and Christmas season. The Twelve Days of Christmas come to an end on the morning of January 6.

According to the *Merriam-Webster Dictionary* epiphany means (1) a usually sudden manifestation or perception of the essential nature or meaning of something, (2) an intuitive grasp of reality through something usually simple and striking, (3) an illuminating discovery, realization, or disclosure, (4) a revealing scene or moment.

In the Christian tradition Epiphany means the manifestation of Christ to the gentile world. In Jesus God has revealed himself and has made known his love to the entire world. He has demonstrated his desire to have a relationship with every last one of us.

Epiphany remembers the coming of the wise men bringing gifts to visit the Christ Child. By so doing, the magi reveal Jesus to the gentile world as Lord and King. Sometimes the day of Epiphany is referred to as Three Kings' Day.

Following the old custom of counting the days of Christmas beginning at sundown each day, the evening of January 5 is the Twelfth Night. It is a night for feasting in some cultures, which includes the baking and presentation of a special King's Cake. In New Orleans, a King's Cake is also part of the observance of Mardi Gras the day before Ash Wednesday.

On January 6, Saint John's Lutheran Church in our town has, in years past, gathered to light an Epiphany bonfire. They collected discarded Christmas trees to use as fuel for the occasion. The fire symbolized the arrival of Jesus as the light of the world.

The Episcopal Church of the Advent, also in my hometown, follows a prescribed litany for the Festival of Light. In the exposed beams above the chancel in the sanctuary, a star is permanently affixed. On Christmas Eve through Epiphany the star shines brightly above the altar.

The account in Matthew's Gospel of the arrival of the wise men in Bethlehem is the basis for Epiphany.

> After they had heard the king, they went on their way, and the star they had seen when it rose went ahead of them until it stopped over the place where the child was. When they saw the star, they were overjoyed. On coming to the house, they saw the child with his mother Mary, and

they bowed down and worshiped him. Then they opened their treasures and presented him with gifts of gold, frankincense and myrrh. (Matthew 2:9-11)

The Gospel of Luke gives another account of the way God revealed himself in incarnation. About forty days after the birth of Jesus, Mary and Joseph took their baby boy to the temple in Jerusalem to be consecrated. The aged Simeon, just and devout, had no uncertainties as he cradled the infant Christ in his arms.

> "Sovereign Lord, as you have promised,
> you may now dismiss your servant in peace.
> For my eyes have seen your salvation,
> which you have prepared in the sight of all nations:
> a light for revelation to the gentiles,
> and the glory of your people Israel." (Luke 2:29-32)

Serving in the temple was Anna, an eighty-four-year-old widow. "Coming up to them at that very moment, she gave thanks to God and spoke about the child to all who were looking forward to the redemption of Jerusalem" (Luke 2:38).

Simeon and Anna, both elderly, were among the very first believers. They experienced a personal epiphany no less significant than that revealed to the magi.

Our Epiphany observance may be in the context of a congregation, or it may be in solitude. My favorite Epiphany story is *The Other Wise Man* by Henry Van Dyke (Harper & Brothers, New York, 1923). The story begins,

> You know the story of the Three Wise men of the East, and how they travelled from far away to offer their gifts at the manger-cradle in Bethlehem. But have you ever heard the story of the Other Wise Man, who also saw the star in its rising, and set out to follow it, yet did not arrive with his brethren in the presence of the young child Jesus? Of the great desire of this fourth pilgrim, and how it was denied, yet accomplished in the denial; of his many wanderings and the probations of his soul; of the long way of his seeking and the strange way of his finding the One whom he sought — I would tell the tale as I have heard fragments of it in the Hall of Dreams, in the palace of the Heart of Man.

The Other Wise Man is a riveting story. It gives a perspective on Epiphany that extends far beyond January 6.

Another Epiphany resource that is meaningful to me is the Christmas carol "We Three Kings." The lyrics tell the story of the magi, the star that they followed, the gifts that they brought, and the baby that they found.

> We three kings of Orient are,
> Bearing gifts we traverse afar,
> Field and fountain, moor and mountain,
> Following yonder star.
>
> O star of wonder, star of night,
> Star with royal beauty bright,
> Westward leading, still proceeding,
> Guide us to thy perfect light.
>
> Born a King on Bethlehem's plain,
> Gold I bring to crown him again,
> King forever, ceasing never,
> Over us all to reign.
>
> Frankincense to offer have I,
> Incense owns a deity nigh,
> Pray'r and praising, all men raising,
> Worship him, God most high.
>
> Myrrh is mine, its bitter perfume
> Breathes of life of gathering gloom,
> Sorrowing, sighing, bleeding, dying,
> Sealed in the stone-cold tomb.
>
> Glorious now behold him arise,
> King and God and sacrifice,
> Alleluia, alleluia
> Earth to heav'n replies.

Three prayers in the liturgy for Epiphany from the *Book of Common Prayer* have become a part of my personal Epiphany observance.

I.

Father, you revealed your Son to the nations
by the guidance of a star.
Lead us to your glory in heaven
by the light of faith.

We ask this through our Lord Jesus Christ, your Son,
who lives and reigns with you and the Holy Spirit,
one God, for ever and ever. Amen.

II.

Father of light, unchanging God,
today you reveal to men of faith
the resplendent fact of the word made flesh.
Your light is strong,
Your love is near;
draw us beyond the limits
which this world imposes,
to the life where your Spirit
makes all life complete.
We ask this through Christ our Lord. Amen.

III.

O God
Who on this day
through the guidance of a star
didst manifest
thine only begotten Son to the gentiles;
mercifully grant
that we who know thee now by faith,
may one day be brought
to the contemplation of the beauty of thy majesty.
Through the same Christ our Lord. Amen.

* * * *

39.
THE EPIPHANY STAR

Perhaps you will not be surprised to learn that over the years some have called me Captain Kirk. Being identified with the *Star Trek* hero is not all bad. Captain James T. Kirk and the crew of the *Starship Enterprise* captured the hearts and minds of multiple generations.

Star Wars created additional fans who explored galaxies far, far away from a darkened theatre while eating popcorn and gazing at the silver screen. The popularity of these fantasies is indicative of the fascination humans have with the stars.

Epiphany has been called a day for stargazers. It is a time for those who face darkness by looking for the light, even the light of a single star. The magi from the East were neither the first nor the last of those who are drawn to the mysteries of heavenly lights. Native Americans looked up to observe the constellations they named Big Bear and Little Bear. Ancient Greeks on the other side of the globe also peered skyward into the night, giving those constellations the same names, Ursa Major and Ursa Minor.

Stargazers are dreamers. Copernicus faced the darkness of ignorance and declared our star, the sun, is the light at the center of our universe. Galileo offered a new vision of creation. As a result, he was vetoed by the darkness of the Inquisition.

The magi of ancient Persia were dreamers and stargazers. They were probably members of the Zoroastrian religion. They believed the heavens mirrored the events on earth. These wise men from ancient Persia gazed into the sky and saw an unusually bright star. They believed it was a sign that a royal person had been born. Following the star, they traveled to Bethlehem to honor the child and to offer tribute. This is the stellar event that we commemorate on Epiphany.

I, too, am a stargazer. Twenty years ago I traveled with a group of Boy Scouts to the high mountains on the border between North Carolina and Tennessee. Troop leaders had planned the trip to help younger scouts learn camping and cooking skills. One young man was overjoyed with the prospect of grilling over an open fire and baking in a cast-iron Dutch oven. He was so eager to prepare food that he forgot to pack one essential item for the trip.

At bedtime, I knew something was troubling him. As darkness settled over the mountains, the night air turned cold. The young boy huddled near the campfire and became very quiet.

"You need to get some sleep if you're going to do all of that cooking tomorrow," I advised.

"I forgot my sleeping bag," he said sheepishly.

This was not my first experience with young scouts. As a grizzled old leader, I was prepared. I offered the lad my sleeping bag, which he accepted gladly. I retired to my pickup truck in the parking area only two hundred yards away.

I grabbed a foam pad and a couple of tattered fleece blankets from a stash behind the driver's seat in my truck cab. I made a comfortable pallet in the bed of the truck and stretched out for the night.

There at the trailhead on top of a mountain, I had a magnificent view of the night sky. There was no moon. Neither were there any ground lights to dim my view of the heavens. I was perfectly oriented beneath Polaris, the North Star. When I awoke throughout the night, I tracked the procession of constellations around the Pole Star. The Big Bear, the Little Bear, Queen Cassiopeia reclining on her couch, King Cepheus, and Draco the Dragon moved in a close circle at the top of the sky. Further down the heavens, other constellations rose into view and then dipped out of sight. On this spring night I saw Orion and his dog, Taurus the Bull, Cygnus the Swan, and the Gemini Twins.

The stars have always fascinated me. Once in August, while at the beach, I had a clear view of the night sky. I knew it would be the perfect time to witness the impressive display of a meteor shower. The moon was in the first phase. On Sunday night, I walked to the end of a long boardwalk. There were no clouds, and the moon was faint. The stars were bright. A little after midnight, the show started. I stretched out on the wooden deck listening to the ocean and gazing into the dark sky. The sea breeze was refreshing; the meteor shower was spectacular. As it turned out, that was the only clear night for viewing the stars while we were at the coast that year.

I remember standing on the tailgate of a sports utility vehicle (SUV) with a pair of binoculars on a cold February night in 1986, straining to see Halley's Comet near the peak of its most recent pass of earth. The Comet was visible for about one week, so two nights later I took my children out in the middle of the night to see it. We could faintly see the cosmic traveler just above the horizon. If you missed it, don't worry. Halley's Comet will return in July 2061.

Just eleven years after Halley's Comet zipped by, Hale-Bopp made a grand appearance. I saw the comet clearly from the Morningside Baptist Church parking lot during the daytime in the spring of 1997. If you missed Hale-Bopp, I'm sorry. It will be back again in 4385.

These celestial sights pale in comparison to what the ancient magi must have seen. The star compelled them to follow. It must have been something to behold!

The stars fascinated a young man named Edward who was born in Marshfield, Missouri, in 1889. Edward majored in math and astronomy in college. He graduated from law school and became a practicing attorney. He got bored after just a couple of years and decided to pursue a graduate degree in astronomy. He focused his research on nebulae, distant objects in the sky that couldn't be categorized as stars. He moved to Pasadena, California, to work at Mount Wilson Observatory with the world's largest telescope.

Edward made discoveries that revolutionized the field of astronomy. He identified a pulsating star in the galaxy Andromeda. Until that time, scientists believed that the Earth's galaxy, the Milky Way, was the only galaxy in the universe. The Milky Way, they thought, measured only about 100,000 light years across. Edward's discovery proved that the universe was billions of times larger than scientists had thought.

Edward devised a system to classify galaxies based on their shapes. In 1929, he made what is considered his most important discovery. He developed a mathematical formula that led to the conclusion that the universe is expanding.

In 1990, four decades after Edward's death, the National Aeronautics and Space Administration (NASA) launched the Hubble Telescope, the first telescope based in outer space. It was named for him, for Edward, Edward Hubble. The telescope captures accurate images of faint, distant objects. Photographs taken from the telescope have expanded scientific knowledge of the universe. Even more, the Hubble Telescope has increased our sense of wonder about the stars.

Because of my interest in stargazing, my dad gave me a telescope for Christmas when I was a college student. I have kept the gift on a closet shelf, taking it down only occasionally. The instrument is not easy to set up and is somewhat difficult to focus.

I wanted my children to see the moons of Jupiter. I set up the telescope in the driveway, found Jupiter, found four of the moons, and let each child take a turn looking through the eyepiece. Everybody had a turn, but Erik took an exceptionally long time gazing at the big planet.

"Erik, do you see Jupiter?" I asked.

"Yes, and I see the moons, too."

"What are you looking at so long?" I inquired.

"I'm just waiting for something to happen. I might discover something new."

The shepherd boy David was a stargazer. He spent long hours through the night protecting the flock and watching the constellations circle Polaris. David was also the sweet singer of Israel and a song writer. Psalm 8 is among his best known poems, especially among stargazers.

> O Lord, our Lord,
>> How excellent is your name in all the earth!
>> You have set your glory above the heavens!
> When I consider your heavens, the work of your fingers,
>> The moon and the stars, which you have ordained,
> What is man that you are mindful of him?
>> And the son of man that you visit him?
> For you have made him a little lower than the angels,
>> And you have crowned him with glory and honor.
> O Lord, our Lord,
>> How excellent is your name in all the earth! (Psalm 8:1, 3-5, 9 NKJV)

* * * * *

40.
PERSONAL EPIPHANY

The pages of the Bible are filled with epiphany moments. God is in the business of revelation. He is constantly making himself known in one way or another. The manifestation of God's presence is found in a burning bush at the foot of a mountain and in a thunderstorm on the mountain peak.

The season celebrated in this book is imbued with stories of the presence of God:

- Gabriel's unsettling announcement to Mary
- The vivid dreams of Joseph
- The startling appearance to the shepherds
- The star of Bethlehem faithfully leading the magi to Jesus

When I was a seminary student, I read Lewis Sherrill's book *The Struggle of the Soul.* Sherrill wrote about three different ways to approach life's journey.

First, some people live as if they are on a treadmill. Life for them is meaningless, without purpose. Burdened by toil and labor, they feel they are going nowhere.

A second way is to view life as a saga, to regard our experiences as a series of adventures and ourselves as tourists. That way of living gives us no sense of direction, no integrity. We spend our time merely searching for the next pleasurable experience. Life as a saga is, as Shakespeare wrote in Macbeth's soliloquy,

> Tomorrow, and tomorrow, and tomorrow,
> Creeps in this petty pace from day to day,
> To the last syllable of recorded time;
> And all our yesterdays have lighted fools
> The way to dusty death. Out, out, brief candle!
> Life's but a walking shadow, a poor player,
> That struts and frets his hour upon the stage,
> And then is heard no more; it is a tale
> Told by an idiot, full of sound and fury,
> Signifying nothing. (William Shakespeare, *Macbeth*, Act 5 Scene 5)

Third, we may embrace life as a pilgrimage. John Bunyan's classic allegory, *Pilgrim's Progress*, illustrates this path. It is what Robert Frost and, later, Scott Peck called "the road less traveled." This is the way Christians are to live. The Apostle Paul says that we are growing into the fullness of the stature of Christ. We are constantly moving in the direction toward becoming more like our Lord.

Each one of us has significant epiphany moments along the path of life. If, as Christian pilgrims, we believe that God has a plan, we will learn to be alert for his intervention in our lives. People who are on a pilgrimage have a destination. Though they will not necessarily have a clear vision of the entire venture, they do have a sense that God is leading their lives. Jeremiah expressed this in a message he delivered on God's behalf. It is God's word for all of us today as well. "'I know the plans I have for you,' declares the Lord, 'plans to prosper you and not to harm you, plans to give you hope and a future'" (Jeremiah 29:11).

If we are searching for meaning and purpose in life, along our way we will have interactions with others who are our traveling companions. When viewed as a pilgrimage, life takes on a greater sense of God's direction and God's leading. Certainly that has been the experience in my life.

With that in mind, I want to share four of my personal epiphany experiences with you.

* * * * *

41.
EPIPHANY AT CROFT

The Apostle Paul coined the phrase "the church in your house" (Phile-mon 1:2 NKJV). The term is an apt description of the Christian home in which I was reared. My mother believed that God intended for her to have a large family. Her desire was to have twelve children. Dad promised Mama she could have as many as she wanted. God blessed them with eight. I am the oldest.

In our home the Bible was opened and read aloud every day. We had family prayers morning and evening. Each child was assigned scripture passages to memorize. Singing hymns and speaking about spiritual matters was common-place. In time, Mama started a Good News Club in our backyard. Neighborhood children gathered for her homebaked cookies and lemonade. Using a flannel sto-ryboard with cut out figures, she told them the stories of Jesus. Only heaven knows the number of children who first professed their faith in our backyard.

When I was two years of age, my parents were members of First Baptist Church in Spartanburg, South Carolina. Dad and Mama were asked by that church to start a mission in an old army chapel at Camp Croft on the out-skirts of Spartanburg. With a few volunteers, they cleaned out the aban-doned military building, made the needed repairs, and dedicated the refurbished sanctuary.

Before long, Dad started leading Sunday morning worship services. He did everything. He served sometimes as janitor and sometimes as pastor. He was the Sunday School Director, Chairman of the Deacons, and Music Director. He basically took on any job necessary to help the mission.

Mama's job was to lead in the nursery at the church. She had earned a degree from Winthrop College in Early Childhood Education, an academic major she designed. She wanted to share her gifts by ministering to children, including her own. Mama and Dad had a clear division of labor in the church, as was their pattern at home.

Wofford students Bill Lancaster and Jack Nanny served as the first two pastors of that small church. After the church had grown, Allen Smith, a young man just out of seminary, was called to be the pastor. One Sunday morning, he gave an invitation. With all heads bowed and all eyes closed, he said, "If you would like to accept Jesus as your Savior, raise your hand."

My good friend George was sitting next to me on the pew. He was about two years older than I was. George elbowed me, "If you'll raise your hand, I'll raise mine."

I took the dare and raised my hand. George did not raise his hand.

The pastor saw my hand and said, "I see your hand. Is there another?"

He did not call me forward. Instead, he asked Mama and Dad for permission to talk with me privately. I met with the pastor in his study on a Wednesday afternoon. After asking me several questions, he gave me the opportunity to accept Christ as my Savior. I was seven years old. I really did want to ask Jesus to come into my heart. It was a happy decision. On that same Wednesday night, wearing my Hopalong Cassidy jacket, I walked down the aisle at Croft Baptist Church and made my public profession of faith. A few Sundays later, I was baptized by Reverend Smith.

A year and a half later, an evangelist from Texas preached at Croft Baptist Church. Evangelism means sharing the good news of Christ. My favorite definition of evangelism is one hungry person telling another hungry person where he found something nourishing to eat.

Instead, the Lone Star State parson delivered only bad news. This preacher fit most of the stereotypes we might have of stem-winding revivalists. As he admonished the congregation, he paced back and forth across the platform. He screamed at the top of his lungs and shook his pointy finger like a Colt revolver. He literally preached hellfire and damnation, terrifying me and a host of others. He accused us all of being despicable backsliders.

On Sunday night we went back to church. The evangelist had a film for us, a flickering movie of Hades. It didn't occur to me at the time to ask how he obtained the horror flick from hell. I realized much later that his film probably contained scenes of bubbling mud from Yellowstone National Park or geysers spewing hot water and steam out of the ground. I remember one particularly vivid scene of the lake of fire, a dark picture showing floating dead bodies within a blaze as intense as a flaming oil spill in the Gulf of Mexico.

Obviously, this product of cinematography was terribly frightening for an eight-year-old boy. For the next several years, when I ran a high fever, I had recurring nightmares of that lake of fire.

By the time the ranting preacher extended the invitation that night, I was sobbing. A master at implanting doubt about whether believers really were Christians, he repeatedly asked accusingly, "Do you know that you have really been saved?"

I hurried forward at the invitation, weeping profusely. Almost every person in the church moved to the front of the sanctuary to make certain of their salvation. The only people who did not come forward were my parents and the pastor and his wife. The evangelist had troubled a lot of people, and I was one of them. I insisted that I needed to be baptized again. Mama and Dad tried to talk to me about it, as did our pastor. I was so adamant that they relented, allowing me be baptized for a second time. I learned later that all of them had been repulsed by the evangelist's strategy.

So, how can my negative experience at Croft be considered an epiphany?

As years passed, I realized that I had been manipulated. The first time that I asked Jesus into my heart and accepted him as my Savior was sufficient. A profession of faith should be a happy experience for a child. God is a loving Father who accepts us just as we are when we come to him. Jesus even insisted that we come to him as little children (Mark 10:15). That experience should never be traumatic.

As I entered my teen years, the residual effect of that one frightening night at church tainted my spiritual development. As time went on, I became more and more resentful of my experience with the evangelist. I determined that I would never again be the victim of religious bullying. I made a conscious decision to never again walk down the aisle of a church in response to a coercive altar call issued by a conniving cleric.

My bitterness after the frightening experience at Croft troubled me for a long time. I have never seen the evangelist again. I don't even remember his name. But I prayed for years that I would be able to forgive him. I beseeched God to hinder him and his tribe from harming others.

I am keenly aware of spiritual abuse. Subverting the grace of God is wrong. I cringe when I hear a preacher planting seeds of doubt in a person's mind about the security of salvation.

Flannery O'Connor wrote a novel about religious pathology. The name of her book, *The Violent Bear It Away*, was derived from a statement by Jesus who said that from the beginning until now "the kingdom of heaven suffers violence, and the violent take it by force" (Matthew 11:12 NKJV). There are still those who do violence to the gospel. O'Connor shows the harm that can be done through spiritual bullying. When evangelism becomes bad news instead of good news, then violence has been done to the gospel.

Later, as I responded to God's call to pastoral ministry, I determined that I was not going to have any part in spiritual abuse. The Apostle Paul expressed a similar conviction:

> We have renounced disgraceful ways, secret thoughts, feelings, desires and underhandedness, the methods and arts that men hide through shame; we refuse to deal craftily, to practice trickery and cunning, or to adulterate or handle dishonestly the word of God, but we state the truth openly, clearly, and candidly. And so we commend ourselves in the sight and presence of God to every man's conscience. (II Corinthians 4:2, Amplified Bible)

I regard the experience I had at Croft as an epiphany because it had direct and lasting impact on my sense of call to pastoral ministry.

* * * * *

42.
EPIPHANY OUT OF AFRICA

My parents and my grandparents laid a firm spiritual foundation for me. My mother and my grandmothers, Mammy and Granny, were all students of the Bible. These three women firmly believed in the importance of memorizing Bible passages. Two verses were the basis for that conviction. One was, "Thy word have I hid in mine heart that I might not sin against thee" (Psalm 119:11 KJV). The second was, "Thy word is a lamp unto my feet, and a light unto my path" (Psalm 119:105 KJV). All three women were convinced I should memorize scripture by heart. They were even willing to bribe me to memorize Bible verses. On the day I stood in her kitchen and quoted word-for-word the entire Sermon on the Mount (Matthew Chapters 5, 6, and 7), Mammy gave me a ten-dollar bill and a big slice of warm apple pie topped with vanilla ice cream.

Every summer Mama gave each of her children several verses of scripture to learn by heart. The summer before I was in the seventh grade, she assigned the following passage to me.

> I beseech you therefore, brethren, by the mercies of God, that you present your bodies a living sacrifice, holy, acceptable to God, which is your reasonable service. And do not be conformed to this world, but be transformed by the renewing of your mind, that you may prove what is that good and acceptable and perfect will of God. (Romans 12:1-2 NKJV)

I memorized those words from Saint Paul and could recite them whenever Mama asked.

The following summer she gave me exactly the same scripture to memorize.

"But I already know it," I protested.

"Kirk, you know the words. You can say them. But I want you to know them in your heart."

The summer before the ninth grade, Mama gave me exactly the same passage.

"Mama, I know those verses."

"Yes, Kirk. Now I want you live by them."

I have often heard people talk about having a life verse, one passage of scripture that has influenced them more than any other. I have been reluctant to identify a life verse. Those verses can change from time to time. I suppose if I had to identify life passages, those verses from Romans would be among them.

My dad and my grandfather told me the stories of the Bible. My earliest memory of any religious experience is my dad telling me the story of Gideon. He said, "I want to tell you about a man who won without fighting." The account of Gideon was so fascinating to me that I could hardly believe that it was in the Bible. My love for storytelling comes right from this story-sharing heritage.

I learned from my family that spiritual formation begins at home. It is where we first learn to pray, to cherish the Bible, and to give tithes and offerings to God. More children accept Christ at home than anywhere else.

When I was in the seventh grade, I started working at our family business. The lumberyard, too, was a place of spiritual development for me. I learned that every person is important. I learned the value of simple honesty. I learned to tell the truth, especially when it meant admitting my own mistakes. I learned that work is a noble endeavor.

I also absorbed many practical lessons during those summers. Back in those days anyone could get a driver's license at age fourteen. I learned to drive a three-ton lumber truck. I enjoyed working with men I admired: Pappy, Dad, and my uncles. I enjoyed talking with customers and hearing their stories.

Most of all, I learned that I didn't have to work at a lumberyard very long before I heard the Lord calling me to do something else.

When I was in the ninth grade, I became a Sunday School dropout. Two things happened. First, I saw my Sunday School teacher at a restaurant one Saturday night behaving in a way that did not square with his teachings. Secondly, my grandfather had a stroke and was unable to drive his car. My grandmother suffered from asthma and was a shut-in.

On Sunday mornings, I walked the half mile to Pappy's house and drove him to church. Instead of attending my age-appropriate class, I accompanied my grandfather to his Sunday School class. Dr. Jim Turner, a religion professor at Converse College, taught a class of older men. I was privileged to learn from a scholar. He taught the Bible to those elders as rigorously as he taught his college classes. I give Dr. Turner much credit for helping me fall in love with the Bible. His teaching gave me the desire to learn all I could about God's Word.

The year I graduated from high school, I spent the entire summer in Africa, in what was then Southern Rhodesia, visiting my aunt and uncle who were missionaries. I saw something there that was appalling to me: *apartheid*, severe, harsh racial discrimination.

Growing up in the South, I had attended public schools that were completely separated, black from white. Movie theaters, swimming pools, and restaurants were strictly segregated. Public establishments had three restrooms: men, women, and colored. Usually there were two carefully labeled water fountains: white and colored. Black passengers always rode in the back of city buses and in separate cars on passenger trains. Racial discrimination was the norm where I grew up. There were no exceptions. Like so many white Southerners, I was totally blind to the gross injustice of this system.

When I returned from Africa, it was as if scales had fallen from my eyes. I could then see the prejudice around me. I did not talk about that realization often, but I pondered it deeply. I can see now that God was preparing me. I was taking another step forward in my pilgrimage.

My grandfather had been very sick that summer. After being in Africa, I began spending most nights at the hospital, talking with Pappy. I learned a lot about the experience of dying from him. I discovered that people die pretty much the way they live.

Intent on being a doctor, a medical missionary, at that time, I entered Furman University in the fall. My plan was to major in biology and minor in chemistry. Three weeks after I began college, my grandfather died. His death was a severe grief experience for me. Pappy taught me how to cuss and how to pray. His prayers came straight from the heart. He spoke to God the way he spoke to everybody else. He didn't put on any airs. Praying was not about flowery language. Pappy was reverent, but he figured neither he nor God had time for prattle. His earthy spirituality has been a continuing influence in my life.

That summer I gained insight into the nature of prejudice. I also learned about the mystery of death. Those were personal epiphany experiences for me.

* * * * *

43.
EPIPHANY AT RIDGECREST

When I was a freshman at Furman University, the director of the Baptist Student Union (BSU) was on my case all year long, pressing me to join the BSU. I visited a time or two, but I wouldn't join. The group seemed to have a holier-than-thou attitude that was offensive.

As I was growing up, Mama and Dad knew the wisdom of letting me make my own decisions. By the time I got to college, decisions about where and when I went to church were entirely mine to make. I don't think there was ever a time when I breathed a sigh of relief and said, "Free at last! Free at last!" Coming into the freedom of my adult years had already happened gradually.

One day at the end of my freshman year, the BSU director came up behind me in the Post Office. I was checking my mail one final time before leaving campus for the summer. He put his hand on my elbow and said, "We are having an end-of-the-year BSU retreat this weekend. We would like for you to go with us to Ridgecrest."

I paused just for a moment. All of my stuff was already loaded into the car. I was ready to leave campus for the summer.

I said, "Well, okay. I'm all packed. I don't have a thing planned for the weekend. I'll just drive to Ridgecrest, not ride the bus, and I'll work out my own place to stay." I was still holding back.

When I got to Ridgecrest, I found that the BSU had rented a big house where everybody was staying. I had already had plenty of opportunities to be in a big house with a lot of people when I was growing up. That was called home! I chose instead to stay alone in a small, secluded cabin owned by my Uncle Tom.

About forty members of the BSU had spaghetti for supper that night. I took one look at the retreat leader and thought, *I just don't want to spend my weekend listening to this guy.*

I volunteered to wash all of the dishes, so that I would not have to attend the session that evening. My wife can attest to the fact that this behavior is out of character for me. From my post at the steel kitchen sink, I could hear the students singing. As I scrubbed the dirty pots and pans, I could hear the speaker holding forth, sounding so much like an evangelist. I was glad I was in the kitchen.

After I had washed all of the dirty dishes, pots, and pans covered with greasy spaghetti sauce, I slipped out the back door. I climbed the hill to my uncle's cabin and soon fell asleep.

Sometime during the middle of the night, I had an experience with the living Christ. I can't tell you whether I was awake or asleep. I can only tell you that it was very vivid and very brief, maybe ten to fifteen seconds. I saw the face of Jesus. It was unlike any representation I have ever seen of him before or since.

Christ Jesus asked me a question. "Kirk, are you willing to do what I want you to do?"

"Yes, Lord," I answered, and that was it. Christ disappeared from view. He was no longer visible. Then I experienced overwhelming peace.

I have never seen him again, not like that. But, I've known that he is always with me, ever present, but out of sight.

The next morning I went to the Sunday service in the main auditorium at Ridgecrest. I do not remember the preacher or the sermon topic, but I do remember the invitation. "If you are willing to do what Jesus wants you to do, would you come forward?"

I had vowed never to walk the aisle in a worship service again. But, how could I not come forward for that invitation? I had resisted all these years, but I had made a promise to Christ the night before. I got up out of my seat in the balcony, came down the front, shook the preacher's hand, and told him, "I am willing to do whatever Christ wants me to do, but I have no idea what that is."

He said, "We have counselors waiting for you."

I went out a side door of the auditorium and down a long hall lined with small rooms, each with an eager face peering out, waiting to counsel me. I walked past them all, hurried back up to the cabin, made two peanut butter and jelly sandwiches, threw them in a backpack, and climbed to the top of Rattlesnake Mountain. I found a comfortable place to sit on a flat rock. Mount Mitchell rose above the Blue Ridge far in the distance. I watched the clouds blowing across the wide sky. I listened to the wind.

I told God, "Lord, I don't know what you want me to do, but I am willing to do it." I sat on the rock most of the afternoon, but I heard not one mumbling word from God.

I waited on the mountain until I was sure the BSU had loaded on the bus and left for Furman. Then I hiked back to my uncle's cabin where I spent a peaceful night.

Early the next morning, I drove to my home in Spartanburg. When I walked into my mother's kitchen, Gertrude Kelly, a black woman who worked for Mama on Mondays, was standing there. She turned to me and said, "Kirk, we want to have a Bible school at our church, but we ain't got no preacher. Would you come do Bible school for us?"

White college students did not do Bible school in black churches in Spartanburg, South Carolina, in 1963. The next week, though, I led Bible school each day at Allen Chapel Methodist Church. The first day, about fifty kids attended. I played my guitar, told the Bible story of Gideon, and played several Boy Scout games.

Every day, more and more kids came. I found it necessary to recruit parents and other members of the church to help. By the end of the week, 125 kids had attended. Throughout the entire week, I was the only white person there.

The last day, a big car pulled up in the church yard. A large black man in a three-piece suit got out and walked over to me. He said, "Reverend Neely..." I looked around to see who he had in mind. That was the first time I had ever been called "Reverend." He continued, "We want to have a Bible school at our church, too. Would you lead one for us?"

Two weeks later, I was leading Bible school at Chestnut Ridge Methodist Church. Two or three weeks after that, I was leading Bible school at Mount Zion Methodist Church further down Highway 56.

Right after I returned to Furman in the fall, I ran into the president of the BSU. I had just registered for classes.

She asked, "What happened to you? The dishes were so clean! We saw you walk down from the balcony and come forward Sunday morning. We looked for you afterwards, but no one could find you. What happened?"

I explained, "I just had a few things I needed to work out."

"I'm so glad I ran into you! We have a big problem, and we need your help. The Reedy River Baptist Association wants us to lead a Backyard Bible Club in a housing project. We are scared to death."

I asked, "When do they want you to have this club?"

"Tuesday afternoons."

I looked at my course schedule and saw that I had biology and chemistry labs on Monday, Wednesday, and Thursday. Nothing had been scheduled on Tuesdays, so I told her I would help. I knew exactly what to do. Every Tuesday afternoon, I helped the BSU lead a Backyard Bible Club in a housing project in Greenville.

I discovered that it was not necessary for me to know God's entire plan for me. I just had to be willing to do his will. When you tell God that you are willing to do what he wants you to do, he will show you. He will not reveal the whole plan at once, but he will direct your next step.

That fresh insight becomes an epiphany moment every single time.

* * * * *

44.

EPIPHANY AT HAZELWOOD

To this day, I regard Furman University as holy ground. Located in Greenville County at the foot of Paris Mountain, Furman offers a picturesque campus with beauty beyond description. The liberal arts education I received at Furman left me longing for more. It was at Furman that I met and fell in love with Clare.

Furman was a challenging arena of intellectual growth for me. The Furman faculty was populated with outstanding teachers who were marvelous examples of a balanced blend of faith and reason. Dr. Gordon Blackwell was installed as President of Furman while Clare and I were there. In his inaugural address, Dr. Blackwell said, "We will seek the truth wherever we find it. We will not fear the truth, nor will we turn away from it. We will follow the truth wherever it leads." Clare and I have adopted that as a benchmark for our lives.

Furman was also a place of spiritual growth for me. The annual Religious Emphasis week gave us the opportunity to interact with outstanding spiritual leaders. I first meet Dr. Carlyle Marney at Furman. He was an iconoclast if ever there was one. It was at Furman that I first heard Dr. John Claypool preach. He would later become our pastor in Louisville and my professor of preaching.

My time in Africa had implanted in me a desire to be a medical missionary. I applied to medical school during my senior year at Furman. This was the height of the Vietnam War. The medical university had many times more than the usual number of applicants, many seeking to avoid the draft.

I learned that I could not enroll because the state legislature had instructed the school not to accept anyone who did not plan to practice medicine in South Carolina. I had written on my application that I intended to be a medical missionary. The Dean of the Medical University told me I was disqualified. His decision may have been a severe mercy. The truth was that while I had done well at Furman, my academic record might not have been good enough to qualify anyway. In any case, I was distraught, heartbroken.

My religion professor Dr. Theron Price had nominated me for a full scholarship to Princeton Theological Seminary. I had turned it down because I wanted to go to medical school. Understanding my disappointment, Dr. Price advised me to attend seminary for a year since I planned to be a medical missionary and then to reapply to medical school.

I was furious. I did not want to go to seminary, but if I intended to go to the mission field, I needed to have at least one year of theological education. I applied late to Southern Seminary and was accepted immediately. I registered for all academic courses: Greek, Hebrew, New Testament, Old Testament, biblical archeology. I took none of the classes about running a Sunday School or preaching sermons. I just wanted to be a medical doctor and a missionary.

When I discovered that I had to do fieldwork, I delayed signing up as long as possible. Other students were working in churches. But, that was the very last thing I wanted to do.

Clare and I lived in an apartment in Seminary Village. The place was crawling with roaches and preacher boys. We got rid of the roaches. The preacher boys were more pervasive and irritating. I just did not see myself as one of them.

Late one night, I stood in the middle of the apartment complex. I shook my fist at heaven and declared, "I will never be a preacher!" I have deleted the expletive I used when I addressed the Almighty that night.

On the day of registration for classes, Dr. Wayne Oates, the professor working the line, asked, "Mr. Neely, you do not want to be here, do you?"

I answered, "No sir, Dr. Oates. I don't want to be here at all."

"Well, here you are, and we are sending you to a hospital to work as a chaplain for your fieldwork."

Little did I know then that Dr. Wayne Oates would become my mentor. He supervised my clinical counseling work and my Doctor of Ministry program. In 1972, we wrote a book together, *Where to Go for Help*. I could not see it then, but God was preparing my way at every turn.

I finally accepted the fact that I was required to do fieldwork. Being a hospital chaplain was my best option. I found some comfort thinking that working in a hospital might give me an opportunity to meet some physicians. Maybe they could help me get into a medical school. Alas, all the doctors were from other countries and could barely speak English.

I was assigned to Hazelwood Tuberculosis Hospital. Every patient had either contracted tuberculosis as a result of residing in the Ohio River Valley or developed black lung disease from working in the dusty coal mines of Kentucky.

Every week I went to the hospital. I fulfilled my fieldwork obligation. I fussed, and I fumed. I chafed, and I bristled. I went through the motions until the day I walked into a ward where three Baptists and one Roman Catholic gentlemen were patients. I stood by each bed, making a perfunctory visit to the three Baptists.

I had learned quickly that in a hospital setting being a Baptist was helpful. The only patients who ever asked what denomination I was were the Baptists. Most everyone else was just glad to have a minister at their side to pray with them.

After visiting the three Baptist men, I walked over to the little Roman Catholic man, Mr. Droughter. His body was ravaged by tuberculosis. He was reduced to skin and bones by this wasting disease. With a ring of saliva dried around his mouth, he used all the breath he could muster to whisper, "Sir, what is your mission?" I was stunned. I talked with him a bit, had a quick prayer, and left the hospital.

I began the drive back to our apartment in Seminary Village. Zipping around the expressway, I kept returning in my mind to Mr. Droughter's unusual question. Back at home, I went through my regular post-Hazelwood routine of disinfecting my shoes and taking a shower. Clare and I enjoyed lunch together. We talked about the question that was stirring my soul.

That afternoon, I pondered and prayed about Mr. Droughter's question. I picked up a book I had been assigned to read, *The Minister and the Care of Souls*, by Daniel Day Williams. An insight from Williams made a lasting impression on me. He said it is in the actual practice of ministry that the pastor meets the living Christ. When we minister, we encounter Christ in our lives. Jesus said, "Inasmuch as you did it to one of the least of these my brethren, you did it to me" (Matthew 25:40 NKJV).

I felt compelled to talk with Mr. Droughter again, so I drove all the way back across Jefferson County to the hospital. When I walked by the nurses' station, one who knew I had been in earlier that day asked, "What are you doing back here?"

When I told her that I had returned to see Mr. Droughter, she said, "You're too late. He died about an hour ago."

A question asked by a dying man became my call to Christian ministry. "Sir, what is your mission?" The whispered question from the lips of a man at death's door is the reason I have been a pastor for forty-five years. Mr. Droughter helped me realize that God had placed me in the middle of a hospital full of suffering and perishing souls. They needed a pastor as much or more than they needed a physician.

I had been marking time, waiting to get to some other place to do what I thought God wanted me to do. Instead, God had taken me to a place I did not want to be to show me what He had planned for my life. I wish I could tell you that I have never looked back. But, I have. I have second-guessed myself, but I have never regretted my decision.

Regardless of the number of times we shake our fist at heaven and curse, regardless of our resistance, regardless of our intentions, we must listen to God's plan. It is better than our own. "Therefore, if anyone is in Christ, he is a new creation; old things have passed away; behold, all things have become new" (II Corinthians 5:17 NKJV).

Becoming a new creation happens when we realize that God is breaking into our lives to impart new revelation. It may be a dawning awareness that gradually becomes clear, or it may be a sudden insight that surprises us. When we pay attention to God's leading, the next step on our path is illuminated.

I have noticed that when God has something to say to me, he often puts it in the form of a question. Sometimes the question is posed by another person. Sometimes it is a still, small voice. Rarely has it been a direct confrontation, but it did happen once.

"Kirk, are you willing to do what I want you to do?"

"Sir, what is your mission?"

"How can you expect to be a father until you learn to hurt?"

God knows that I am wired to ask questions, so he turns the tables and questions me. I have learned that I must pay attention. Most of the time I do. And those are moments of personal epiphany.

* * * * *

CONCLUSION

Somewhere in the process of putting this book together, the question came to me, "Kirk, why is this book important?" That's another question!

When the dog days of summer are ended, evening arrives earlier, a chill is in the air, and our senses are quickened; we are able to open our lives to new possibilities. We anticipate the arrival of the season celebrated in this book.

Thanksgiving beckons us to a deeper sense of gratitude. The attitude of thanksgiving prepares us to open our hearts to God's stirrings. In Advent we join Mary in expectantly preparing to receive Immanuel into our hearts. Christmas reminds us that God continues to grace us with his love. And so it prepares us for the New Year. Epiphany brings the season to a close, yet we go forward with the awareness that God repeatedly reveals himself in our lives through experiences of personal epiphany.

I could continue through observance of Lent, the celebration of Easter, and the joy of Pentecost. But, that is another book for another time.

Until then, maybe these chapters will inspire you to preserve your own holiday stories and memories. Write them down in a journal or a notebook. Record them on video or on compact disk. What better holiday gift could you give your children and your grandchildren than a permanent record of your personal epiphany?

As you prepare that present for your family, my hope and prayer is that this book will be a blessing to you, and that the holidays will bring the blessings of God to you and your home.

Faithfully,
Kirk H. Neely
May 2011

ACKNOWLEDGEMENTS

I am thankful to Michael Smith and his predecessor Carl Beck, Editors of the Spartanburg *Herald-Journal*, for giving me the opportunity to write many of these columns and the permission to publish them in book form. In a time when hometown newspapers are stressed and in transition, it is gratifying that there is still a place in print for a weekly column like "By the Way."

I am grateful to Jeff Zehr and his predecessor Landy Timms, Editors of *H-J Weekly*, for their trust and their competence. Jeff and Landy are evidence of the friendships that can develop between editor and writer.

The story "Christmas at Croft" originally appeared in *Hub City Christmas* published by Hub City Writers Project in 1996. It is used here by permission.

"Jason's Story" was included in *Hidden Voices*, a book edited by Kristofer M. Neely, published by The Hub City Writer's Project, and sponsored by Piedmont Care, Inc. and The Arts Partnership of Greater Spartanburg. It is included here by permission.

Emory Cash has provided the illustrations for *Santa Almost Got Caught*. As a life-long doodler, I am amazed when a talented artist like Emory, using simple pen, pencil, and ink, can be so creative.

I am thankful every day for Kathy Green, a secretary and colleague. She has read the entire manuscript many times making helpful corrections and suggestions. Kathy is simply the best.

I am indebted to the people of Morningside Baptist Church. As a pastor, I could not write without the encouragement and support of a congregation that understands writing as an extension of ministry. This book, in particular, has been a work of faith undergirded by prayer.

My writing would be diminished without Clare, my wife and my companion in all things. Her beautiful eyes can spot a misspelled word or a punctuation error at twenty paces. But she constantly reminds me that no matter how many times a manuscript is edited, every reading always discloses further errors. If you, the reader, find a mistake, please let me know. We'll fix it in the next edition.

After I write "By the Way" each week, Clare is my first and most perceptive reader. In a very real sense, to have my name on a piece of writing is to have her name on it, too. She pushes me to do my best.

Our children — Mike, Erik, Scott, Kris, and Betsy — have been my first listeners. Down the years, they have served as a sounding board around the family table, by the hearth, on the back porch, and at bedtime for most of these stories. I am grateful for their patient attention, intelligent encouragement, and loving advice. You have always been a great audience!

I especially appreciate the time and effort our daughter Betsy and our son Scott spent editing this manuscript. Their work made it a much better book.

Finally, I am deeply indebted to those who read what I write. Without you, these words would fall silent. Through you, they carry the ring of truth far beyond my keyboard.

Thank you. Thank you. Thank you. Thank you, all.

❈ ❈ ❈ ❈ ❈

ABOUT THE AUTHOR

Kirk H. Neely is a native of Spartanburg, South Carolina, and the oldest of eight children. Kirk grew up on the lumberyard, a family business operated by his grandfather and his father. He draws from these experiences in his storytelling and his writing.

Kirk was coauthor with Wayne E. Oates of *Where to Go for Help*, Westminster Press, 1972. The Hub City Writers Project published *Comfort and Joy: Nine Stories for Christmas* in 2006. *When Grief Comes: Finding Strength for Today and Hope for Tomorrow* was published in July 2007 by Baker Books. *A Good Mule Is Hard to Find and Other Tales from Red Clay Country* was published by Hub City Writers Project in 2009 and was selected as a finalist for the 2010 SIBA Awards for the best in Southern literature. *Banjos, Barbecue, and Boiled Peanuts* will be released by The Hub City Writers Project in October 2011.

Kirk received a Bachelor of Science degree from Furman University in Greenville, South Carolina. He received the Master of Divinity Degree and the Doctor of Ministry Degree in Pastoral Counseling from The Southern Baptist Theological Seminary in Louisville, Kentucky. He was named a Merrill Fellow at The Divinity School of Harvard University.

Since 1996, Dr. Neely has served as Senior Pastor of Morningside Baptist Church in Spartanburg, South Carolina. He is a frequent speaker at storytelling festivals, corporate and private functions, and family life programs throughout the Southeast.

Neely is a writer for the Faith and Values page of the Spartanburg *Herald-Journal*. He writes a weekly column, "By the Way," for *H-J Weekly*. As a freelance writer Kirk's articles have appeared in several periodicals including *The Spartanburg Magazine* and *Sandlapper Magazine*. He has also written two books of family genealogy, *Neely Cousins* and *Hutson Heritage*, each privately published. Two devotional books, *By the Sea* and *Unto the Hills*, were published in 1996 by Christian Supply Company.

While a student at Furman, Kirk met Clare Long of Leesville, South Carolina. They were married in 1966. Kirk and Clare live in the home built by his grandparents after the Great Depression in 1937. Kirk is a Master Gardener and enjoys working in his own garden. Kirk and Clare are parents of five children. They have eight grandchildren.

CPSIA information can be obtained at www.ICGtesting.com
Printed in the USA
LVOW11s1325090215

426275LV00003B/135/P